PRAISE FOR INVISIBLE THINGS

"Tina Quinn's simple, courageous sharing of her stories reminds us of the invisible beauty and power behind all our lives."

~ **Steve Chandler,** author of *CREATOR*

"*Invisible Things* is a timely reminder that despite outward appearances we are all deeply connected to one another. Tina Quinn's personal stories and insights on relationships, meditation and personal growth help us explore our lives in new ways. Now more than ever the world needs a deeper sense of compassion and connection. *Invisible Things* invites us to nurture these feelings in ourselves, and to share them with the world."

~ **Peggy Callahan**, CEO and co-Founder Voices 4 Freedom

"When we worked together at Sustainable Conservation, Tina Quinn helped me approach environmental problems with openness. Now, in *Invisible Things* she takes this a step further by illustrating beautifully how openness and presence help us embrace the challenges and joys of our lives—and experience the poetry of being."

~ **Frank Boren,** Past President, The Nature Conservancy

"In her inspiring book, Tina Quinn empowers us to harness our creative power and become our best selves by slowing down, listening, feeling more light and questioning our thinking. Through powerful stories she reveals how invisible things are always there supporting us. A terrific guide to living a healthier, more open-hearted and joyful life, and to helping those around you do the same."

~ **Christine Porath,** TEDx speaker and author of *Mastering Civility: A Manifesto for the Workplace*

"Tina Quinn has created a body of work that can open us up to noticing all the little *Invisible Things* here to help guide us on our path through life. She pours her heart into every story as she shares her practical guidance and wisdom. This book will capture your heart, mind, and soul. It will leave you in greater inquiry about what is possible."

~ **Karen Davis,** co-author of *Unconventional Wisdom* and *When All Boats Rise*

"Everyday experiences take on elements of the sublime in *Invisible Things*. Reading it is like sipping a cool glass of water on a hot summer day or enjoying a warm cup of tea with your best friend. Tina Quinn brings a soothing yet sparkling perspective to the art of living a good life, making visible the invisible forces that shape each day. Her stories invite feelings of light, joy and possibility into your life."

~ **Caroline Leach,** business owner, author and speaker on social media branding for careers and companies

"Tina is a remarkably creative coach and a compassionate guide to the wonders of life."

~ **Jason Goldberg,** author of *Prison Break*

"In *Invisible Things*, Tina Quinn shares her life with openness, vulnerability and honesty. Her stories are gripping, heart-warming and humorous, and they guide us to see life differently. She provides both practical and spiritual tips and tools to elevate our lives. I couldn't put it down!"

~ **Kamin Samuel,** business & life coach, author of *Increase your Abundance Starting Today!*

"Full of wit and truth, *Invisible Things* takes us on a well-crafted adventure, offering the reader a glimpse into the unseen forces that impact our daily lives. Tina Quinn pours her heartfelt and hard-won experience into this masterpiece, and through authentic and brilliant storytelling she allows us to awaken to the beautiful music of our soul. This book is a must-read for anyone ready to take their own personal journey of self-acceptance, inner peace, self-love and service."

~ **Devon Bandison**, author of *Fatherhood is Leadership*

INVISIBLE
THINGS

Dearest Nayla
You inspire me
and so many in
This world. So
grateful That we
are on this life
Journey + so
amazing to watch
You grow + glow
along The way.
Love you tons.
XO
Tina

INVISIBLE THINGS

The most important things in life
are the ones you can't see.

TINA QUINN

HIDDEN WISDOM PUBLISHING

~ To ~

John, for your love, friendship and unending support.

Mom, for being my greatest teacher and cheerleader.

TABLE OF CONTENTS

FOREWORD

I've read a lot of books by a lot of consultants, coaches and psychologists over the years and the rare thing—the most unusual and exciting thing—is when the author and the book are a perfect match, when there's no difference between who the author really is, and what their book is.

This is one of those books—written by the extraordinary life and leadership coach, Tina Quinn.

It lines up. It's that perfect match. The same unassuming, vulnerable, passionate and compassionate qualities that set Tina Quinn apart as an effective, transformative coach are also right here in this book.

With authors in the personal development field you usually get the other thing. Coaches and public speakers tend to load their books up with second-hand stories, motivational theories, already-popular ideas and borrowed opinions. In their books you get what they *think*—or what they think you should think—but not how they really experience life.

My own books have often erred in that direction, which is

why I'm so envious and impressed by what Tina Quinn has delivered to us with this book.

As I was first reading her intimate stories and deeply personal experiences I was almost tempted to look over my shoulder to make sure no one would catch me reading someone else's private diary.

So when you read her stories, some painful, some joyful, you'll feel you've been welcomed into her world and can share in all the emotions that give it life and color.

Reading this book reminded me of my years in my twenties when I was trying to make my living as a sportswriter. I had always admired (and tried so hard to follow) the words of sportswriter Paul Gallico, who wrote, "It is only when you open your veins and bleed onto the page a little that you establish contact with your reader."

You'll feel that contact throughout this book of illuminating stories. Tina has courageously and skillfully done that, and one stands amazed that she did it in her first attempt at writing a book!

She tells us here that she has a quote up on the wall in her office in her father's handwriting. It's a quote from Adlai Stevenson (who was Governor of Illinois, twice nominated by the Democratic Party to be their presidential candidate and later appointed by President John Kennedy to be the U.S. Ambassador to the United Nations). You'll read his full quote in her book ahead. But I think it's worth looking at now. Stevenson says he considers "experience" to be a knowledge "not gained by words, but by touch, sight, sound, victories, failures, sleeplessness, devotion, love."

Those words up on Tina's wall must have made their way

into her mind, heart and spirit because they describe her life and work—and now this inspiring book—just perfectly. His quotation finishes by gently advocating, ". . . a little faith, and a little reverence for things you cannot see."

That sets the tone and the underlying theme for this entire book. And it does so without really trying, without obvious calculation. It's just there: the faith and the reverence for things you cannot see. This theme builds from story to story, from experience to experience. It reflects Tina's own reverence and faith, Tina's own devotion and love, for things you cannot see. If you have the same experience I had during this entertaining book, you might find that your own faith and reverence have been touched and nourished and expanded.

I'm just guessing here about the degree of impact that quotation had on Tina's life and book. Just as I was just guessing years ago when as a newspaper reporter I got to spend a full day interviewing a young Arnold Schwarzenegger as he was conquering the international bodybuilding world and the world of action movies. He said he grew up with the words "Joy Through Strength" up on a wall in his boyhood home in Austria.

Sometimes words have a magical, life-changing impact for people. It's clear that Tina Quinn wanted to do for her readers what her father's hand-written words did for her.

In the beginning of the book, Tina tells about her early-life failures and frustrations, as she was looking for love and fulfillment in all the wrong places until she reached out in desperation to a counselor who helped her wake up to a new life. She writes about the turnaround this way: "I started to believe that the universe was a place that supported me instead of something I needed to muscle through." And that then she

". . . began to notice the good things I wanted more of in my life and to make choices based on what I wanted to create instead of simply reacting to what I thought society wanted me to have and do."

To me, these were the invisible things she couldn't see before. The deeply felt sense that the universe was a place that supported her, and that there was, inside of her, the previously unseen capacity to create what she wanted to create.

You'll find other invisible things throughout this book, but those were the two I felt the most. I noticed that all the invisible things in this book emanated from the creative power of love itself. They are also both spiritual and real-world practical. Like her very funny story of how she created her own birthday celebrations after realizing it was the perfect solution to feeling they had been under-appreciated in the past. Why wait for the world to catch up with what you see as possible to create?

That real-world practicality permeates these stories of living from the heart. We learn what happens when you apply love to situations most of us would just feel like victims of. And they also give us a clue as to why Tina Quinn is such an effective coach of other people and leaders in organizations. Yes, she's spiritual and lovingly empathetic. I don't know anyone who connects with people so soulfully from the moment they connect. But she's also a truth-teller and can deliver radical wake-up calls to people who are selling themselves short and not realizing their own creative powers. This is the Tina I know in the world of leadership and coaching and human performance.

My unexpected delight comes from the fact that she has successfully captured the unseen spiritual underpinnings of her day-to-day creative energy in this book. And she's done it not through theories or philosophizing but by the simple, courageous sharing of stories—by which I mean the sharing of life experiences, true events, one after another, that each brought more and more light to her own understanding of the invisible power and beauty behind her life. And she shares it in such an unassuming, almost heartbreaking way, that we ourselves, as grateful readers, get that she wants us to experience the same invisible things, and is devoting her life to helping that happen.

Steve Chandler
Birmingham, Michigan
2019

What is essential in life is invisible to the eye.

Mr. Fred Rogers
Won't You Be My Neighbor?

— INTRODUCTION —

INVISIBLE THINGS

We are all connected, not just to the people we know, but to all the energy in the universe. What are some of the invisible things that tie us together? Love, grief, curiosity and wonder—to name a few. But there are so many more invisible, ineffable mysteries that connect and sustain us. Although we cannot always capture them with words or thoughts, we feel them deep within and all around us as we experience the miracle of our lives.

As a coach, I am privileged to have clients share their lives with me. In these pages I'm sharing *my* life with you in the hope that you may see yourself in my stories and take away something of value. Perhaps you'll even catch a glimpse of what's possible for you, and of your own invisible connections to the most meaningful things in life.

ON
GROWING UP

— 1 —

Searching for Happiness

There is a crack, a crack in everything.
That's how the light gets in.

Leonard Cohen

The story of my dad dying and me being lost was like an outfit I couldn't change. Every decision I made, every conversation I had and every belief I held during those first five years after his death were defined by that singular story.

Eventually I woke up one morning and questioned the truth of the story, and this began my road to change. But before that change—and my freedom—I looked everywhere outside myself for happiness and peace.

I never questioned my accomplishments in life because it always felt like I was on the path I was destined to follow. Finishing high school, graduating from college, playing sports, working at a variety of jobs, dating different people and spending time goofing around with friends was all part of this unformulated plan. It was a very smooth and comfortable existence. Society told me what success looked like and I followed the socially acceptable path without too many detours.

When my dad died suddenly from a heart attack on the tennis court, it was the unexpected bump in the road that threw me completely off course, and I didn't know how to find the path again. Never again would he be able to help me with my life decisions. I was terrified because I still had so much to learn from him and so many questions that I needed answers to.

Without my dad as my guide, now what? What's the next step for me? Do I stay in the relationship I've been in for the past five years? Do I live with my mom? Where do I work?

And then bigger life questions . . . *What is happiness and how can I find it? What do I value in life and why? Why do I even care?*

These are important questions for all of us at any time in our lives, but at twenty-two, I believed that my dad could have answered them for me—if only he were still alive.

I had graduated from college the month before and I knew I needed to pay my bills ASAP. New York City, where I had planned to live and had partially moved, didn't feel like an option any longer because my mother was alone, so I moved home and took the job I had been offered at a local department store in their management-training program. At work, I could stay busy, make money and be distracted from my questions and mounting depressing thoughts.

A department store is an ideal job for complete distraction because you can work ten to fifteen hours every day and it seems "normal." As management trainees we were convinced we had to work that hard to get ahead, and because we were paid a salary instead of by the hour, we were there all the time.

It was my first full-time job, the people were nice and I learned a bit about fashion—which I had never taken an interest in before. I managed to maintain a few friendships, and I was available to help my mom, but those were very long and exhausting days.

After eighteen months, I was beginning to understand that working non-stop wasn't going to get me the answers to my deeper questions about life and priorities. In fact, despite how great I felt about being constantly distracted, the store wouldn't pay me more than a small salary, and I knew that I had to move on.

Coinciding with my angst at work, my boyfriend and I decided to split up. He had been my partner and friend for so long, but I couldn't make my life work so I concluded that our relationship was part of the problem. Shortly thereafter, one of the senior-level managers at the department store and I became friends. She was funny and charming, and when she asked me if I would be interested in getting involved in an intimate relationship, I was willing.

She and I became romantically involved. We socialized with her friends, took a holiday together and remained in an exclusive relationship for four months. I became immersed in her world and quickly came to realize that the emotional part of being in a relationship with a woman felt similar to being in a relationship with a man, and the expectations were as complex as any relationship I had been in before.

I had speculated that maybe a romantic relationship with a woman would help me feel better about myself because she would understand me in a way that a man never could. In the end, that wasn't true. She was seven years older than me, generous, loving and willing to show me the ropes of this new world, but I was looking for someone to help me get out of my confusion and pain—which put a lot of pressure on both of us. Also, I knew by then that I wasn't attracted to women the way I was to men. What seems obvious to me today—that a deep and wonderful friendship with another woman isn't the same as a romantic relationship—wasn't obvious then. I was trying to find the answers outside of me, from someone else, and that never works well.

A few months later I left the relationship with my co-worker. I also left my mom and the department store and moved from Los Angeles to San Diego to get some clarity. When I arrived, I had a new business idea. I wanted to travel and had recently been certified as a scuba diver. Why not combine two things I was excited about? So I spontaneously approached the owner of a scuba store and asked if he would be interested in having a travel agency in his retail store. It would be a one-stop shop for his clients, offer that extra customer service that would create a competitive advantage for him and be really fun for me—and maybe I would find answers while traveling. Who wasn't happy when they were traveling?

He agreed enthusiastically, and so I traveled, planned scuba tours all over the world for his clients, did a lot of diving myself, saw new places and met interesting people. I started dating a good guy, lived with close friends and exercised often. It was an exciting time, and yet I was still lost emotionally, and those same life questions continued to haunt me.

It took me a year in San Diego to realize that I needed to move back home, figure things out and find a job that paid well. My dad had been in real estate since I was a kid and I knew I could make a good living if I worked hard in that field; consequently that's what I pursued. I think I also wondered whether more money—which I thought would make me relaxed and confident—would be the answer I was looking for.

For two years I worked long hours, put together deals and made better money than I had in all the previous years put together. I was living on my own by then and feeling much more independent. But what started as an exciting career came to an abrupt halt when another, much older and well-connected broker inserted himself into one of my lease negotiations, and my manager instructed me to "let it go." In the end, the other broker took home the entire commission because of his influence in the community (he had played golf with the prospective tenants). The lack of support and the cutthroat nature of this interaction threw me completely off-kilter, and this in turn helped me realize that my values were not aligned with the way the company did business. It made me question whether it was time to get out of the business completely, because by then I had figured out that more money didn't make me happier.

After this, I began working again with Alison, the therapist I had seen right after my dad died, and I started feeling better. The next job I took was working for a local land trust—using my real estate license in support of efforts to create permanent open space in the Santa Monica Mountains.

In the next chapter I'll share in greater detail what happened in Alison's office and how I went from looking outside myself for answers to finding those answers inside me. But what I was already slowly beginning to see was that none of society's messages about what creates a happy life—the perfect job, the most prestigious university, lots of travel, great sex, a flawless body, the best relationship, more money—can satisfy our craving for happiness and peace. No matter how thin I was, how much money I made, who I was having sex with or how much travel I did, I still didn't know who I was. I had been pretending to be someone I wasn't, because that's what I thought I *should* do. My last real estate transaction was the proverbial last straw. It was the motivation I needed to try therapy again. I trusted Alison, and I had experimented long enough to know that it was time to take responsibility for the rest of my life.

Some of my clients today are exploring these same issues, and they are experimenting the way I did so many years ago. Maybe they are a different age and they have checked different boxes: great grades, amazing leadership positions, top-notch colleges, spectacular career performance, perfect resumé or the opposite —and everything in between. Consistently, they all want to know: *What's next? Where can I find happiness? Is this all there is? And what's it all about?*

When we talk together, we question the truth of society's priorities and norms. We examine their own beliefs and values and explore how they can become who *they* want to be.

All of us can create versions of our best selves, and we do that by asking some of the same questions. What are the questions you're asking these days?

— 2 —

WHAT HAPPENED IN ALISON'S OFFICE?

Sorrow prepares you for joy. It violently sweeps everything out of your house, so that new joy can find space to enter. It shakes the yellow leaves from the bough of your heart, so that fresh, green leaves can grow in their place. It pulls up the rotten roots, so that the new roots hidden beneath have room to grow. Whatever sorrow shakes from your heart, far better things will take their place.

Rumi

Alison was the therapist I had seen shortly after my dad's death. At first we worked on simply getting through the dark days because I was so angry at him for abandoning me. I was convinced he had left me completely unprepared for life, and in charge of my mom, my sister and the family business.

For many months I dreamed I was standing on a floating platform, and every time I took a step in any direction, I fell off the side into a free fall with no end in sight. I would wake up with a jolt and realize again that my dad had died—and the path I thought he wanted me to follow no longer made any sense.

I lived in Hermosa Beach while working at the department

store, so when I moved to San Diego I left Alison, therapy and my very confusing relationship behind. Alison and I had been working together for a year by that time and our conversations had been about how to make it through the next day, one day at a time. I lived in San Diego for a year. When I moved back to Los Angeles to work in real estate, I found a new therapist: Paul.

My year with Paul wasn't a healthy therapy relationship because I was looking to him for my answers . . . and he was happy to provide them for me. I finally cut it off when, following a session in which he told me that I was fat and nobody would be interested in me, he suggested we go out to breakfast—and I went! Looking back now, the invitation was wrong for so many reasons, but at the time it felt to me like a social invitation. It made me wonder: were we now friends? Was he asking me out on a date? Was I suddenly thin enough for him to find me attractive? I still remember that breakfast, me nibbling at a muffin thinking about how I couldn't eat food in front of him and how he didn't understand who I was at all.

I never went to another session with Paul because I knew in that moment that I needed to take my life back into my own hands and he couldn't help me do that. Nobody was coming to save me. Having my head in the sand, unconscious, ignoring the truth of my situation, thinking someone or something had the answers to a happy life—I thought all this would be an easier path to becoming an adult, but it wasn't.

When I walked into Alison's office to start therapy for the second time, I was still terrified that I was never going to feel peaceful, productive or like I had any sense of direction. By that time, however, I was willing to try again, to be uncomfortable and really look at my life and my choices. Thankfully she was there to help.

So how did I begin this journey of waking up, of feeling better and lighter? It's the same thing I work on with my clients today. Alison and I dissected the truth of my situation. She helped me become more accurate, we questioned my thinking, and I began to realize that nobody else was going to make it better. I needed to own my *own* growth for the first time in my life.

We started by examining who I was at work—in my commercial real estate job. I questioned thoughts I had about whether I needed to make a certain amount of money or close a specific number of deals to feel good about myself. In the office I tried so hard to be smart, happy, productive, a "natural" at working with clients and making money . . . and it all felt fake. Commercial real estate is a competitive business, and that's how I believed I needed to act to succeed at it.

I remember thinking that my new eyeglasses were great because they served to separate me from the person to whom I was talking; that way they wouldn't see the "real" me. With Alison we questioned my beliefs and desperation to have people see me a certain way, and I began to understand that that's not the way I wanted to live the rest of my life. I was exhausted spending my days posturing and constantly trying to interpret every situation to see how I should act.

I was Tina, the chameleon.

When I finally recognized that being a commercial real estate broker was a great profession—just not the right one for me—I felt free in a way that I never had before. I began brainstorming jobs with everyone I knew to find something that would be a better fit. Finding out what my core values were, then actually choosing my direction based on those values, took time, but once I began getting some clarity I saw opportunities everywhere.

Work was only the first thing Alison and I examined. Over the next year we looked at relationships, body image, travel and how I was spending my time and money. I compared what I valued in life to what my parents and society valued. It was in those conversations that I began to see what kind of life was possible for me. With Alison's support, I slowly started to change, to try new things, to be more real each day and to experiment with new relationships. It was scary at first, so we questioned my beliefs and moved carefully, and gradually my fears began to disappear. Many of the things I spoke with Alison about almost thirty-five years ago are woven throughout the stories I share in this book.

It was in Alison's office that I started to believe that the universe was a place that supported me instead of something I needed to muscle through. I began to notice the good things I wanted more of in my life and to make choices based on what I wanted to create instead of simply reacting to what I thought society wanted me to have and do. The more I made decisions based on my value system, the better I felt.

~

This week, one of my clients told me that he's been putting armor on since he was seven—thirty years ago—because life's a battle and he needs to be prepared. We started the process of questioning his beliefs, and we looked at a few of his fears. It became clear that despite his prestigious job, he still sometimes operates from a seven-year-old's perspective. After our conversation he was able to see his story differently and felt a sense of freedom. The same kind of freedom I felt when I was in Alison's office.

We can all change, no matter what we've been through or how old we are. It requires a willingness to experiment, ask questions and practice change in small increments . . . and a little faith in invisible things.

— 3 —

UNCONDITIONAL FRIENDSHIP

Don't walk behind me; I may not lead.
Don't walk in front of me; I may not follow.
Just walk beside me and be my friend.

Albert Camus

When I walked into Alison's office the second time, I wasn't even sure it was *possible* to be happy—but I was so tired of being unhappy that I was willing to try anything.

One thing that gave me hope I could change was my friendship with Karen. Karen and I were good friends in high school and spent many days and nights together. We swam in the ocean and skied, went to the movies and did homework; we traveled by bus to each other's homes, laughed, cried and had lots of sleepovers. One of my favorite memories is having delicious breakfasts on Sunday mornings with her family. We went to UCSB together and were roommates our sophomore year.

We had our ups and downs. She tells me that at times I wasn't a very inclusive or generous friend, which is true, and if I'm honest with myself, I knew it at the time. In college there were dinners, parties and beach days where I didn't include her when I could have. As I reflect on those days, I'm embarrassed by that younger, selfish Tina and sorry Karen felt alone some of those times. I am truly grateful we survived those days and that our friendship today is better than it's ever been.

It's hard to explain how important my relationship with Karen was during those crazy years right after my dad died. I shared every detail of my escapades with her and she loved me and laughed with me the whole way through. She never gave me the feeling that I'd disappointed her or that she disapproved of me. She wasn't shocked by my behavior or by my experimentation with sex, relationships or drugs. She accepted my anger, tears and the way I would sometimes isolate myself in my apartment for days. If Karen and I could stay friends throughout what I considered the ugly times, if she stuck around after seeing the worst of me, then I could create my future friendships based on my relationship with her. Having one close relationship meant I could have one more, and then one more . . . and that's the way I would make my new life.

As an example of just how much that friendship meant to me: On my first date with John, who would later become my husband, I remember worrying that the "real me" might not show up and that I would instead default into playing someone I thought he might like. This had been my pattern for many years, and I knew I wanted to change. It didn't take me long to remember that if magic was going to happen between us for longer than this one date, then it *had* to be the real me who showed up—because I would show up as that person eventually anyway. So once again, I used Karen as my point of reference, reminding myself that *she* accepted me for who I was. Trusting to that, I showed up as myself to my date with John; we talked honestly . . . and we connected.

As John and I became more serious, my relationship with Karen continued to be the example of what an authentic relationship could look like. Karen cared enough about our friendship to not only be honest with me, but also to accept my apologies along the way. From there we were both brave enough to talk through her pain and my regret, even though it was horribly uncomfortable at times, and we came out stronger on the other side of those conversations.

But what if Karen had been so hurt by my actions that instead of talking to me, she had held a grudge? That wouldn't have been unconditional friendship, of course, but it certainly would have been her prerogative. She could have kept her pain to herself. I could have decided that I didn't need to apologize because I had done nothing wrong. Instead we put our egos to the side and chose our friendship, and I am so happy every day that we did. *That* is unconditional friendship.

Our deep respect and friendship continue today. Karen is compassionate and clear. She's all about family, friends and service. She is curious and loving, and we're both constantly talking about what's next for each of us. Our lives now have husbands, children, businesses and parents we are responsible for, and we support each other in being the best versions of ourselves throughout all of it. We've lived the past forty-three years embracing each other *because* of our imperfections and our strengths, and we can't hide from each other—which is what unconditional friendship is all about.

My friendship with Karen constantly reminds me that there are invisible forces at work. When we move forward despite being embarrassed by our own actions, when we're willing to do things differently the next time, or when we're okay talking about something uncomfortable and seeing the possibility for change in that conversation, we can cultivate these kinds of deep relationships. If we can remember that we're all learning and growing and trying to do the best we can with the tools we have, life becomes much easier. More love and more forgiveness of ourselves and other people enriches our lives and helps good people find us along our path.

—4—

SOMETIMES WE JUST NEED TO SAY YES

*The old Carl didn't think he was enough for anybody. I thought if
I said yes to things, and got involved with people, then sooner
or later they'd find out I'm not enough. I didn't think I had
anything to share. But now I know that what I have to
share is pretty huge, and I want to share it with you.*

Jim Carrey
Yes Man (film)

Almost six years after my dad's death, I left my commercial real
estate job and used my broker's license to work in the Santa
Monica Mountains as a consultant for a local land trust called the
Mountains Restoration Trust (MRT). I finally made a strategic
move based on my values. It allowed me to combine the skills I'd
developed in commercial real estate with my love of the outdoors
and deep desire to do something to help the environment.

While working at MRT, a close friend asked me to assist him
with a separate real estate transaction. This is where I first
encountered Dan, the owner of the company.

There are certain people you meet along your life path who
can help change your direction—if you're open to possibilities

and are willing to say "yes" without fully knowing what to expect. Dan was—and still is—one of those people for me. He is twenty years my senior, soft-spoken and wise. He owns a successful real estate company, has an incredible marriage and had climbed almost all of the tallest mountains in the world by the time I met him. Dan continues to be a role model of how to remain humble, creative and successful in business and life.

Shortly after our real estate deal closed, Dan introduced me to Frank, his old law partner, although neither was practicing law any longer. Frank is warm, engaging, brilliant and incredibly creative. At that time, he had recently left as President of a large non-profit organization dedicated to the environment and was discussing a new idea with Dan. The project he proposed would combine their real estate knowledge with their passion for the environment, and he assured Dan that they would have some fun together at the same time.

Thankfully, they decided to move forward. When they needed someone to do the day-to-day activities without pay to get the idea off the ground and they approached me, I said YES. They had a great idea and all of us were excited about the possibilities. This project beautifully aligned with my values and experience, and I already had another job paying the bills, so I was willing to experiment and have a new adventure. I kept asking myself, "How much better can it get than to work with Frank, a visionary environmental leader, and Dan, a well-regarded real estate owner and developer?" What an amazing opportunity for growth.

Frank's idea was to bring scientists, business leaders, government employees and environmentalists to the table so that together they could create solutions to big environmental problems. This was a new idea at the time and a brilliant one, too. Before long we had people who had traditionally been on opposite sides beginning to talk solutions before lawsuits.

Once we raised enough money, I began working full-time for our newly formed non-profit organization, Sustainable Conservation, as their first Executive Director. John and I moved to Northern California after we were married, so Frank and I found an office to share in San Francisco. The organization still resides there today. What started as a revolutionary idea almost thirty years ago has developed into an important and much larger non-profit organization that is still creating solutions to tough environmental challenges.

In Jim Carrey's movie *Yes Man*, he plays a guy who is used to saying NO to everything in his life. One day he attends a seminar where he's asked to say YES—to every single thing he can. He agrees, and his life transforms. The message of the movie is extreme but clear: we need to say YES more often. So many times we're waiting to get caught up at work, or we plan to do something special when we have enough money, time, sleep, the right friend or the perfect partner. I said YES to working without a salary with Frank and Dan because it aligned with my values, I was hungry to learn as much from them as I could, I had extra time to work on this project, another job that was paying my bills and I wasn't tied down. I stretched, but not too far.

I said YES.

~

Sometimes I like to ask my clients, "What is something that you can you say YES to right now that stretches you a bit but not too far?" We then talk about what a small stretch might look like in the direction they want to be heading. Sometimes people choose a huge leap to the next job/relationship/event—then get scared, stumble and don't want to try again, or take a long time to recover.

In my case, for example, it would have been a huge leap for me to leave my MRT job the minute Frank and Dan suggested I come work for them, instead of waiting a year. It was really what I wanted to do, but I didn't have enough savings and didn't know how long it would take us to raise the money, so it didn't feel safe. It would have been too much of a stretch at the time and definitely not as fun.

But when we had raised the money to pay me and I could partially replace my income, I knew the time was right to change jobs. That was my "yes-stretch," but it wasn't too far, because I had confidence that we could raise more money within the next six months.

In other words, changing your life doesn't have to be done in leaps and bounds, but can take place one step at a time. A series of small "yes-stretches" does lead to major transformation.

—5—

WHY THE ENVIRONMENT?

From my perspective, I absolutely believe in a greater spiritual power, far greater than I am, from which I have derived strength in moments of sadness or fear. That's what I believe, and it was very, very strong in the forest.

Jane Goodall

Friends sometimes wonder why I have spent most of my life driven to protect the environment. I am constantly thinking about how to integrate the environment into any project, how to bring more clean water and clean air to our communities, how to make sure that people have access to open spaces and how to educate our children about the value of the natural world.

In nature there is profound peace, love, calm, beauty and connection to an invisible, powerful, universal energy. When you're outside, you can hear your own voice more clearly and see that we are but a small part of Mother Earth. My dream is to give everyone an opportunity to experience the natural world.

I have been trying to do this since I was young. Our family home was close to the Santa Monica Mountains. We grew up hiking, camping and backpacking with family and friends. We slept under the stars and woke up to the sounds of the birds and the rushing river. We hiked on the trails, collected tadpoles (pollywogs), watched the sycamore trees wave in the wind and listened to the stream flowing through the canyon. There was a sense of calm I felt outdoors that I didn't feel anywhere else. All my senses came alive with the smell of wet moss, the crinkle of leaves when I walked, bugs I could examine, sunlight as it filtered through the trees and the taste of fresh stream water. I felt small compared to the vast, wild spaces. Being outside gave me faith in invisible things and a connection to a higher power that I didn't understand—but which I knew was there. Even at a young age, I knew the outdoors was where I felt like my true self, and I wanted more of that feeling.

When I talked to Alison and slowed down enough to ask myself what I truly valued, I began to realize how important it was for me to take care of our open spaces. Even at that time I was convinced that the more people we could expose to nature, the better our world would be.

My deep desire to introduce people to the beauty of the remote mountains led me to a transformational college class when I was only nineteen years old. We learned about the plants, animals, history of the surrounding Santa Barbara mountains and the emotional and life-changing benefits of being in the wilderness. One requirement of the class was to put these lessons into action. To this end, Mary—a good friend and fellow classmate—and I created a program to take a group of four, fourteen- and fifteen-year-old juvenile inmates and a security guard on an overnight in the Los Padres National Forest. This was a big deal for them and for us.

In preparation, we went into the jail and taught these boys—who had been specifically chosen for this adventure—about different plants, animals, types of terrain, physical necessities and survival skills. They were very excited and cooperative; we were, at first, apprehensive. But as we learned about the safety details, answered their questions and saw firsthand their openness to this new experience, we were all in.

The day we spent hiking with these young men was another confirmation of the awe-inspiring, transformative, invisible power of the environment. Clean air, physical exercise and no input from the outside world all played a part. Interestingly, if we just looked at the facts of what happened that day—we lost our way, the security guard couldn't keep up so it was just the two of us with the boys, we ran out of food and at points all of us were truly scared—we would miss the most important lessons the boys learned: to trust each other, to have a sense of confidence (which came from problem-solving and bushwhacking their way through the chaparral) and to know the joy that comes with waking up to another world they didn't know existed. Mary and I had a renewed sense of awe experiencing the power of green, open, rugged spaces to inspire and calm all of us.

Being outside, whether in the remote mountains, at a local park or on a trail near our home, makes us humble, grateful and aware of a world bigger than our own back yard. In my discussions with Alison I finally became aware that being outside served as my connection to Spirit, and as a consequence I have devoted much of my last forty years to helping others have their own such experiences.

In my lifetime, I have witnessed what is possible when people put their minds to something and stay with it. In the fifties and sixties, Los Angeles had some of the dirtiest air in the world. Sea life, including kelp, had almost disappeared from our local patch of ocean. Today our air is cleaner and there are dolphins and kelp in the Santa Monica Bay. That kind of progress gives me hope.

After parties in college I would gather huge bags of aluminum beer cans and deliver them to the recycling center, filling the trunk and back seat of my car to the brim. Today recycling is familiar to most people in the U.S. We have curbside trash and recycling pickups, and students are learning about the lifecycles of commercial products in their classrooms. That too gives me hope.

I'm now at that age when many young people longing to help the environment want to meet with me and eventually find a job in the environmental space. They want to learn how I "did it," how I'm so connected and why I keep wanting to help everyone see the value of our environment. As my coach Steve Chandler says, the solution is simple. You must give time and attention to whatever you want to accomplish. I've given a lot of time to helping our environment whenever and wherever I can.

When I'm outside, I am fully alive. The outdoors is a place of infinite love, infinite possibility, and divine connection. If you haven't had an outdoor experience yet, there's a trail not too far from your home. Go curious, with an open mind, and see if you can feel invisible things waking something up inside you.

— 6 —

NERVOUS OR EXCITED

Every act of conscious learning requires the willingness to suffer an injury to one's self-esteem. That is why young children, before they are aware of their own self-importance, learn so easily; and why older persons, especially if vain or important, cannot learn at all.

Thomas Szasz

My mom had some great ideas that I'm just beginning to recognize—which is funny, because I'm fifty-six and she's ninety-three.

When I was in elementary and middle school, tennis was my sport. The tennis club was where my parents spent their free time, which meant that my sister and I spent our free time there as well. As we got older we helped in the tennis camps we'd participated in for years, and we began playing in tournaments.

Competition can be exhilarating and exciting, and when I first started playing in tournaments, it was *really* fun. But as time went on and I played in higher levels of competition, my desire to win became more intense, and I became more serious. I dreamed about the matches before I played. I created each point in my mind, envisioned what the score would be after that point and then how the game and match would turn out. Many times the score was just what I had imagined.

After a few years, however, I wanted to win so badly that the pressure became suffocating. It was terrifying to lose because I believed that each game I lost defined me and showed everyone that I wasn't a "good enough" athlete. When I lost I felt as though I were *that* girl—the one with so much natural talent and possibility who wasn't living up to her potential. I was being crushed under the weight of this thought. I'd go to bed the night before a match telling my mom how nervous I was.

Her go-to response was this: "Oh, Tina, instead of nervous, that's what *excited* feels like."

When I look back at this now I see how brilliant it is. If only I had listened more closely as a teenager and stayed with it longer.

The first time she said it, I remember it being a revelation. Being nervous or excited was a choice I had, and I believed her that I was excited. This brought the fun back into the game for me. I didn't take it so seriously when I was *excited* to play. Every time I would think the thought that "I'm nervous about a game"—or about a talk in front of the class or a conversation that I needed to have—I heard my mother's voice and remembered that I was excited, and that's a great feeling.

This lasted until I was about fourteen years old when, like many rebellious teenagers, I changed my mind about my mom and was convinced that she didn't really know what she was talking about. I *knew* I was nervous. In fact, I felt so nervous that I wasn't going to live up to my tennis potential that I decided to stop playing all together. At the time I told people that volleyball was more fun than tennis, so I'd quit to join the volleyball team. The real truth was that I couldn't handle my frustration and disappointment in myself, and the anxiety I felt every time I even thought about playing was enough to stop me in my tracks.

In my innocence, I pushed myself to be the best I could be and then felt nervous when I didn't think I'd get there. So it seemed a better option was to just stop trying. My mom and I can laugh about this today, but what if I had understood as a teenager what she'd been trying to help me to see? What if I could have had *new* thoughts—that I was exactly perfect the way I was, and that it was fun and *exciting* to compete? What if I knew that losing a match didn't define me or what I would be able to do in life? What if I thought it was a great feeling and I wanted more of that because I knew it meant that I was growing?

What I didn't know then but understand better now is that when something is fun or exciting for us to do, we do it more. And the more we do something the better we get at it, and the better we get at it the more fun it is.

These days, many of my clients and friends say they're nervous and don't want to fail at whatever they're working on. That makes perfect sense, because for most of us it's uncomfortable to fail. But what if we saw failure as simply being one step closer to getting better?

Our lives can change when our thinking changes. Today when I feel that familiar sensation, just asking myself whether I'm excited or nervous is enough to help me see my situation differently and slow down my immediate response. That's usually all it takes for me to try again.

Recently I spoke at a large event as part of my role as Board

Chair at UCLA's Institute of the Environment and Sustainability (IoES). Even though I often speak in front of groups, this was my last event as Board Chair and I put a lot of pressure on myself to make it the *best*, most meaningful talk I've ever done in that capacity. I was feeling nervous. On the way to the event someone asked whether being Board Chair of such a wonderful place was an exciting position to hold and I burst out laughing. I knew in that moment that I wasn't nervous but excited about my talk and the possible impact I could have. Knowing that excitement makes me perform at my best, I was able to show up relaxed and to have fun connecting with the audience.

Is there something in your life that you're feeling nervous, worried or anxious about? Could you consider reframing it for yourself like my mom did for me so long ago? Even if it's tiny, see if you can find something in your situation to be excited about instead. Once you do that, your whole world looks different.

—7—

WHAT IF . . .?

*The real voyage of discovery consists
not in seeking new landscapes but in having new eyes.*

Marcel Proust

A few years ago I was being coached by one of my peers. I told him of my frustration with something my mother was up to and explained that I was "having to" pick up the pieces. I told him the reason I had been taking care of my mother for the past thirty-three years was because my dad used to tell me that if anything happened to him, I was very capable and needed to take care of my mother, who would need help. This coach asked me some simple questions that knocked me off my chair:

"*What if* your dad didn't mean to give you that job? *What if* he changed his mind? *What if* you misunderstood what he was saying and he didn't really mean that at all?"

My world was rocked, because I had never considered that I was living in a story I had created for myself—one that might not even be true.

Growing up with an older father was both wonderful and

challenging. Rudi was fifty-four when I was born and one of the true joys in his life was having two girls. I think having a boy in America seemed like too challenging a prospect for him. He was from Vienna, Austria, an only child raised by his grandparents and born in 1907, when Austria was part of the Austro-Hungarian Empire. After playing professional soccer and working as a travel agent, he traveled through Europe and India and landed in the Far East at the beginning of WWII. In 1945, he moved to America from Shanghai, became an American citizen, fell in love with my mom and created a life that he treasured daily, which of course included me and my sister. He treated us like angels, charmed our friends with his European ways and disciplined us with a rolled-up newspaper. His German accent was so strong that many of my friends couldn't understand what he was saying, but they loved his generosity and passion for life.

Because he was older, we had many conversations about how I was the responsible one in the family. He said that this was a part of the oldest child's job description. He was acutely aware that he was the sole provider for the family and also the age of a grandfather, so he would frequently tell me that if anything happened to him, I would be responsible for emotionally supporting my mother and sister.

We had this conversation often enough that when he died I was wholeheartedly convinced I was in charge of my mother's well-being and happiness. My sister, Kym, was incredibly self-sufficient and although my dad had told me otherwise, I realized that she didn't need me to take care of her. In fact, she soon moved to Boston for work, then graduate school. She met her future husband Mark there, and so Boston became her home. I stayed in Los Angeles, partly because I wasn't sure what to do next and partly to help my mom. At the time my mom seemed incredibly lost without my dad, and I was ready to step in.

Looking back, I can see that my mom was fifty-eight years old, smart, capable and very independent. But we all—even mom—believed a story that she couldn't do it on her own, partially because my dad had reinforced that idea for so many years. So my sister and I became her friends and confidants. We talked about real estate, the stock market, friends, travel, the current events around the world and politics.

In those early years after my dad passed, and as my mother was figuring out life on her own, my sister and I talked through business decisions and details of her personal life with her. As she's aged Kym and I have taken on more and more responsibility for her well-being, which is more typical.

My mom has been a wonderful and integral part of both of our families and has lived a full life. She's traveled with us, spent holidays and Sunday afternoons with us, spent time getting to know our families and has been incredibly generous with all of us over the years, yet sometimes I would hear my dad's voice remind me that I was responsible for her.

For thirty-three years I believed that helping my mom was a promise I had made. I was responsible for her. But what I saw in that conversation with my coach was that this was never true. I had simply never questioned the story that I'd lived for so long. One consequence of this is that I robbed myself of some of the joy of spending time with her because I thought it was an *obligation* instead of a *choice*. But it's *always* been my choice to spend time with her; I just didn't understand that.

Life has been very different since that conversation with my coach. My mom's ninety-three now, and today I'm off to pick her up and take her to get her nails done. I'm not doing this because she needs me to help her, or because it's a commitment I made to my dad, but because I *want* to spend time with her. She's an incredible woman and I am deeply grateful that she's been in our lives for so long.

What if . . .? That one simple question made me see my relationship with my mom differently, and from then on I was free of the story in which I had I felt trapped for so long.

Today when my clients feel stuck, we look together for the stories that are keeping them trapped and then start asking questions: *Is it even true? Was it ever?*

What stories are you telling yourself? What if they aren't true?

— 8 —

LISTENING TO MY FRIEND

*The greatest gift we can offer each other is
the framework in which to think for ourselves.*

Nancy Kline

Many years ago, a dear friend called me to complain about a situation with her business partner. They had been having a disagreement over staffing. From my friend's perspective, she had a lot to complain about. I walked around my house listening to her talk about her situation and kept thinking of great ideas I wanted to share with her. I had so many practical solutions to this problem that I tried interrupting her story a few times.

The conversation didn't go quite the way I expected. After a few attempts to interject ideas, she told me in no uncertain terms that she didn't want me to put a positive spin on her circumstances, tell her why whatever she was going through was really a good thing or even come up with a solution to the problem she was complaining about. The only thing she really wanted from me was to listen to her, acknowledge how she was feeling and let her think for herself.

I wondered (and not for the first time in my interactions with others) how she could not want to see it the way I saw it. I asked myself why *anyone* would want to stay upset about a situation when instead they could see the opportunity in their circumstances, as I did in my friend's. I was convinced that I had the "right" answers for her if she would only listen.

That thought stopped me in my tracks.

How many times did I think I had the right answers for someone—and then actually *stop* listening to them? When I believe I'm right and have it all figured out for the other person, I close myself off to the natural, compassionate nature we all have, and I don't let them do their own thinking. In this case with my friend, I even stopped caring that she was having problems because I had become so frustrated with her same complaint over and over. No further listening or connection with her was possible after that.

Thankfully, she told me what she needed and we agreed that an acknowledgment of how she felt was different from my having the same opinion as her about the situation. She asked me to listen to her *completely* and *not* have a solution. That's challenging if you believe you have the answer, but I cared about the relationship so much that I wanted to change.

From her point of view, the situation was complicated and hard. Not knowing what else to do, I asked her questions about the details. As she considered them she began to realize that she had the answers she was looking for inside her already, and she started to calm down. What she had really needed was just someone to bounce ideas off of. In the end, the complaints ceased and she decided to ask her business partner for a compromise.

~

Complaining has always felt like a waste of precious time to me. It usually only happens because the person who's complaining hasn't created a solution to a perceived problem—*yet*. If I want to help in such a situation, the best thing I can do is deeply listen, acknowledge the feelings that are present, and then ask questions from a place of curiosity.

Many of my clients are frustrated when they *know* they're right about a situation involving their partners, employees, friends or relatives—but the other person won't take their advice. The truth is that we stop listening with compassion when we think we have it figured out for ourselves or the other person.

In the end it is a true honor to be with someone as they think through a problem; it's like watching a flower open to the sun. We can help people think more clearly when we pay attention to them without interruption, listen deeply and ask questions out of curiosity. It's not only fun but it also helps to create a stronger connection, which is one of the best parts of life—that invisible, deep connection with another person.

— 9 —

BIRTHDAY EXPECTATIONS

When we quit thinking primarily about ourselves and our own self-preservation, we undergo a truly heroic transformation of consciousness.

Joseph Campbell

When I was young, my birthday was all about me. This can be typical kid behavior, but I took it to the extreme (which is hard for me to admit today). I believed the way friends and family responded to my birthday signaled how much they cared about and understood me. I expected to be everyone's center of attention. I was concerned about the kinds of gifts I'd get; for example, if someone gave me money rather than a physical gift, I would interpret that to mean that they hadn't spent any time thinking about what I needed or wanted.

When things didn't happen the way I wanted them to, my parents heard about it for days afterwards. Can you imagine the pressure I must have put on them? In fact, sometimes I actually became disappointed *before* my birthday ever happened! I expected them to forget my birthday and not get me a present, and I believed this thought so fully that I lived it regardless of the reality—they had never, of course, missed my birthday.

I hadn't yet learned that life is exhausting and unsatisfying when all we do is think about ourselves and expect friends and family to fall in line accordingly.

When I was thirty-one we moved to Amsterdam—and my world surrounding my birthday opened up. In Holland there's a wonderful tradition where you invite people to your home to celebrate with you on your birthday. But it's not about *you* so much as it is about everyone there—that is, it's about celebrating friendship.

My Dutch friends showed me how they had birthday parties with generosity and grace. At their parties, people sat around the perimeter of the main room, talking, drinking and celebrating together. The host or hostess—the birthday boy or girl—delivered cake and drinks to everyone in the house, and there were frequent toasts to friendship. The parents of the birthday honoree were congratulated for bringing their child into the world. The whole affair was warm, lively, personal—and so much fun.

I decided from that moment forward that my birthdays would be about celebrating friendship and the wonderful people in my life—instead of all about me. Instantly my birthday transformed into a day where I gifted a party *to* my friends. It may sound incredible given what I've shared about my younger self's birthday expectations, but once I decided to turn my thinking from myself to other people, I was happier than I'd ever been on my birthday.

A few years after we arrived back in the U.S., I invited some girlfriends over for a birthday open house in the middle of the day. I asked them to stop by and just give me a hug or stay the whole afternoon, whatever worked best in their schedule. I now do the same thing every year—and I've been doing it for twenty years as of this writing. I ask my friends to bring an appetizer, dessert or drink to share with the group rather than any gifts. The list of women continues to grow, and we keep celebrating friendship.

What a difference it is to live a life where I get to create an event honoring my friendships on my birthday. No more waiting with a long list of exacting expectations for those around me. No more bracing myself for the worst should people "fall short." I went from needing love and appreciation from people *outside* of me to expressing gratitude and giving from the *inside*.

My birthday experience reveals that, like most other things in life, the more we focus on the scared, self-centered parts of ourselves, the less aware we are of the invisible wonders of life— in this case, friendship, connection, and love.

When we expand our focus, removing the emphasis from what's happening to us and transferring the energy away from our worries and fears, we shift to *giving* to everyone around us. I have found life, and birthdays, to be much better that way.

ON
PARTNERSHIP

— 10 —

A NEW KIND OF KNOWING

*Education—a knowledge not gained by words but by touch,
sight, sound, victories, failures, sleeplessness, devotion,
love—the human experiences and emotions of this earth
and of oneself and other men; and perhaps, too, a little
faith, and a little reverence for things you cannot see.*

My dad's adaptation of Adlai Stevenson's address at Princeton University, 1954

It's been almost thirty years since I sat next to John on a flight from Newark, New Jersey, to Los Angeles, California. He and I had both been in New Jersey for different fall weddings and were flying home on the same day. John was seated on the aisle in the middle of the plane and saw me walking towards him. He told me later that he really hoped I would take the seat next to him because I seemed happy and was laughing and talking with the flight attendant as I looked for my seat. I clumsily sat down next to him, shoved my bags under the seat in front of me and turned to him with a big "Hello!" Looking back on it now, I was so fully in the moment, willing to engage with new people and open to whatever life was going to bring me, that in a way it makes sense we connected immediately.

We were relaxed with each other and talked about friends and family, work, exercise and travel. And we had many things in common—both of us had been in New Jersey for weddings, we both lived in Santa Monica a few blocks from each other, we both worked in real estate and we were both reading books by Leo Tolstoy. We had time to get to know each other on our cross-country flight, and we laughed a lot along the way.

Shortly after we took off, I found out that John worked for a real estate development company. Because I wanted to leave my commercial real estate position for something else, we spent part of the flight brainstorming ideas about what else was out there. He offered to introduce me to the property management department at his company, so I innocently gave him my phone number with the intention to keep in touch about job opportunities.

He had a different idea. While on the airplane, he asked me out to dinner. Because I was in a relationship, I declined his first offer. Over the next couple of months John called me a few more times to see if I was interested in doing something together—biking, hiking, dinner or walking on the beach. I still wasn't available, but by that time I had reached out to his company and had a job interview lined up, so I suggested that we have lunch after my interview.

That lunch changed the direction of my work and my current relationship, and it helped to define the rest of my life. For the first time I became aware of a deeper kind of full-body knowing. During the lunch with John, my body was buzzing so much I wondered if they had spiked the iced tea.

By then John knew that I cared deeply about the environment so it made sense that the job in property management that his company had offered me wasn't something I was very excited about. Instead of trying to persuade me to take it, he urged me to think through alternative work opportunities that would combine helping the environment and real estate. We also continued conversations we started on the plane.

Falling in love wasn't on my radar, though the crazy tingling I was feeling throughout my body woke me up to a new possibility. I remember wondering what was going on inside me every time we connected. Because I didn't understand it, I ignored all of my internal signals and continued to say no to John. Fortunately, he didn't give up.

When I broke up with my boyfriend on December 31st, I knew it was time to reach back out to John. I sent him a postcard and asked if he wanted to go for a hike. He called me immediately. Today he tells me that he knew it was "our time" after that. Our first date was to a jazz bar for dinner, and I still remember the orange soufflé with Grand Marnier topping, staying out until three in the morning—and my body buzzing with aliveness at dinner. Nobody else had a chance after that.

I've always wanted to share this story. It's one of my most clear experiences of both the phenomenon of showing up to situations open to possibility—like I did on the airplane—and of knowing that when we slow down and pay attention to our inner signals and the intuition we all have, we allow the universe to help us in unexpected ways.

~

These are things I often work on with my clients. When we slow down and listen to our body's signals, we allow more than just our thinking mind to help us. We pay attention to our inner voice, our higher wisdom, our inner knowing, our intuition. When we give ourselves time to really hear that intuitive voice, our decisions are clearer and more powerful.

Recently a client of mine told me about a date she went on over the previous weekend. She was excited about going out, getting dressed nicely, and going to a restaurant with a man who seemed interesting. She showed up open to possibilities. By the time the food arrived, her inner voice was telling her that the guy she was with felt almost creepy. He asked a few questions that really offended her and the kiss at the end of the evening was uncomfortable. Her inner voice was clear: no interest in another date and there was no romantic connection.

This client had been practicing listening to her body's messages and acting based on them for the first time in her life. It's like learning to drive, and it takes practice. Most of us are instead used to paying attention to our thoughts and talking ourselves out of our feelings. In this case she knew it wasn't right, but she still initially felt disappointed when he didn't want to go out on another date. After we talked about it, she realized that she was more excited about taking care of herself than anything else and was looking forward to another date with a different man.

It took many months for me to recognize my inner voice when I was with John, to understand that the buzzing was my signal that we had an invisible connection and that my body understood this better than my head did. For my client, when we spoke after her date, it was the first time she had an opportunity to reflect on the messages her body was sending her—a full-body knowledge that she had never tapped into before. She told me that she's happy to be learning how to listen to her inner wisdom, and next time she's going to pay more attention and slow down.

(You will find that I talk about "slowing down" often throughout this book. What I mean is that each of us can slow down when we take a few breaths and *choose* how we want to react to an outside stimulus. It doesn't have to be the way we have always responded. When we slow down it gives us a chance to become more aware and thoughtful about our response, and it gives us time to check in with our body's signals.)

— 11 —

TIES THAT BIND US

Let there be spaces in your togetherness. . . Love one another, but make not a bond of love. . . And stand together yet not too near together: for the pillars of the temple stand apart, and the oak tree and the cypress grow not in each other's shadow.

Kahlil Gibran
On Marriage

Happiness and joy in my relationship with John takes honesty, connection, laughter and listening. We have been married twenty-eight years and it still feels like I'm waking up with my best friend every morning. But it wasn't always this way.

John proposed to me on New Year's Eve, 1990. A few weeks later he was laid off when his company downsized. That's hard on anyone, and particularly hard when you are recently engaged. It was hard on me too—both because I felt sorry for him and because I started worrying about our future. I questioned how well I really knew him and wondered whether we'd be able to support a family together.

When he told me that he wanted to wait until after the

honeymoon to get another full-time job, I got scared. What did this mean? I had imagined that we would both earn money to support our future life together and that he was capable of keeping a job to do that. Had I been wrong about him? Would I be supporting the family in the future by myself? Was he not as motivated as I thought he was? I questioned all of it and lived for a while in real fear of our future together.

Our honeymoon plans were to take an adventure trip to Africa, something we had both saved for and dreamed of since we met. He didn't want to miss it and was afraid that if he started a new job before our honeymoon he would be unable to take the time off. He thought we might never have a chance like this again because he too was planning on a future with a family and a serious job.

John moved into my apartment a few months before the wedding and while he was looking for a job, I was working two jobs. The work I was doing was engaging and energizing, but I didn't want to tell John about how great it was for fear that he would feel badly about being out of work, and maybe even jealous of my enthusiasm. By not talking about what was going on with me, I was convinced I was protecting him.

When we met with our minister for our pre-wedding conversation, John and I talked about our future together. I confessed that it was hard to be in a relationship where I was working on concepts that were so exciting and innovative because I couldn't talk about my work.

This came as news to John. He told me that he *wanted* me to share my excitement and stories with him. That's what he thought marriage was supposed to be about, and he had no idea I was holding anything back. He made an important request of me in that moment which I agreed to and still live by today—that going forward I talk to him when something is upsetting so we can catch it early, before it grows into a big, hairy problem in my mind.

When we are in a relationship with someone—parents, partners, kids or friends—so often we are SURE that we know what's going on in the other person's mind. My clients often feel the same way—they are convinced that they absolutely know what their partner, friend or parent is thinking.

In my case, I had created a story that I felt badly for John and I believed that John would feel jealous if he heard how exciting my work was—but the story I created wasn't true. What's more, it was dividing us. I believed these thoughts to be true, and so they made me fearful, upset and distant. In short, they almost broke us up.

On July 6, 1991, we were married, and the minister offered a wonderful metaphor. A marriage, he said, is like railroad tracks, with two solid and separate rails and ties that bind them together. At our best in a marriage, we are two solid and separate people who grow independently of each other. And we create the ties that connect us together and make us happy we're partners. With John and me, some of those ties included our first interactions, where we met each other in laughter, friendship, and in our mutual love of hiking, food and travel. Today there's even more—talking, walking, books, movies, our children, parents— and even some of those poignant but inevitable parts of life, such as health issues and the passing of friends and loved ones. We continue to create new ties each day.

When you look down the railroad tracks into the distance it looks like one track, and that's what it feels like in a marriage as well. We're in it together, as a unit, looking towards our future.

I tell John almost everything now, as soon as I know we need to talk about it, and he still listens to me with an open mind and heart. I do the same for him, and I think it's one of the reasons why we've stayed happy together for so long. Neither of us waits until an issue becomes a "big deal" because it's much better for our marriage and friendship that way.

~

I recently spoke with a client who was having a challenging conversation with her husband. She felt that they were spending so much time taking care of their kids that they had forgotten about connecting with each other. To make matters worse, she didn't want to have a conversation about it because she couldn't think of how they could resolve the issue. She was simply thinking that they were growing distant from each other, and rather than talking about it, she was considering leaving for a while to get some space.

In such an instance, leaving—or just not talking about an issue, pretending it's "not a big deal," which is what I did with John at first—creates a deeper divide than you intend. It takes courage to be open, to have conversations from a place of love instead of fear, and to know that we really don't know what the other person is thinking.

This client and I talked about how to have a loving and honest conversation with her husband, and then we did a role-play based on her biggest fears about how he might respond. As soon as she was clear on how much she loved him and wanted the marriage to work, she was willing to try a new kind of conversation for the first time.

51

— 12 —

JEALOUSY OR FREEDOM?

When we change the way we look at things,
the things we look at change.

Dr. Wayne Dyer

"It's a classic case of jealousy."

I'd just shared a personal story with Kerri Meyers, my first powerful and insightful coach, and I was shocked at her response. All I could think to say was, "I'm not the jealous type. That can't be it." Jealousy made me feel really uncomfortable when I saw it in other people. I always felt it was so painful and unnecessary, such a waste of energy, so I really hated to think that I was jealous.

On that particular Saturday afternoon, just before my call with Kerri, John was walking out of the house to meet friends. I had made a sarcastic remark about him leaving me at home with the kids while he went off to do something fun. After this one call, the rest of my day would consist of driving, shopping and cooking for the family, so I was feeling sorry for myself in that moment. For many years, I'd had a running conversation in my head about what was "fair," and as John was walking out the door, I decided that this definitely *wasn't* a fair split of responsibilities on a weekend day.

What's embarrassing to admit is that John and I had already agreed upon this particular plan. He and I both work hard during the week. Weekends for us are a negotiation: time together—with and without the kids—as well as time apart. The best part of me wants to say "yes" to everything John wants to do, and I want him to do the same for me. Neither of us agrees all the time, but we try to work out our schedules without too much emotion.

But I occasionally found myself making sarcastic comments even after we agreed on a weekend schedule. Earlier that week, when we were in the midst of creating the agreement, I had felt happy that John would be socializing with friends because we trade off over the weekends and it was his turn. But when he was walking out the door, I wasn't happy.

When I make a negative comment, I feel upset with myself and John leaves the house feeling badly. There's no generosity from me and it's probably very confusing to him; one minute I'm okay with our agreement and the next I'm not. This didn't only happen with our weekend schedules; it occasionally appeared in other areas of our lives. When John and I were taking piano lessons together (my idea to have some couple's time) and he sat down to practice, I often felt a twinge of envy if I hadn't done it first. If he and I were heading to bed at the same time but he actually jumped into bed before I did, I would sometimes feel envious because I was still cleaning up or getting organized for the next day.

I didn't behave or feel this way very much of the time and fortunately neither John nor I saw it as a huge problem in our relationship. It was more just a nagging issue that I was ready to get rid of, once and for all, and this coaching conversation with Kerri was my chance.

One of the things I love about coaching is that it offers you the opportunity to question long-held beliefs about yourself and those around you. Sometimes, in a split second, you can see the same situation differently. In the past when I snapped at John, I always told myself I was upset, or angry, or scared. Now Kerri had pointed out another possibility.

Was I simply *jealous*?

Kerri explained that I had a *choice* to feel and act in a way that was more aligned with how I wanted to be. I didn't have to default into a reaction that I didn't like. She said that it wouldn't take work on my part, just a desire to change, awareness, and a new thought.

We talked about how much I deeply love John and want to do anything I can to support the very best life for both of us. Then we looked at the actual situation in detail: John and I had made an agreement in good faith, and I changed my mind. At the last minute I reacted to a thought that didn't serve either of us and dishonored our agreement.

Going forward, I decided that any agreement I made would be something that John, or anyone else, could count on.

From there I chose an alternate thought. Instead of "This is not fair" or "He wants to spend time doing X instead of hanging out with me," I chose: "A good marriage is about both partners living their lives to the fullest—together and apart. We have a great love and a great marriage."

This new way of going about things also required me to be fully aware when I was making an agreement with John. I could no longer say it was okay if I really didn't feel like it was. Recognizing that I had a *choice* in how I responded was huge. I could choose to think good, warm and loving thoughts about John. I could choose to honor my word. I could choose to believe with my whole body that he loved me and that time apart wasn't going to impact that.

One of my clients who has been very happily married for thirty years told me that often when her husband had to work on the weekend, it felt as though he was leaving her to deal with the rest of their family life alone. She didn't like feeling like that.

Once we really looked at the truth of him working on the weekend and at the story she kept telling herself—that she was being abandoned—she realized that none of that story was actually true. In that moment she chose to feel more love and compassion towards him when he had to work on the weekend, and immediately she was free of her story. Sometimes it's like a light switch and you can immediately see life differently, and sometimes it takes practice and happens more slowly. For her it was a light switch moment.

I just received a card from that same client telling me that over the six-month period since we had the conversation, she's never had the thought again and she is closer to her husband than ever. Freedom is when our thoughts no longer create distance with other people, and she is now free in a way that she's never been before.

— 13 —

TELL ME WHAT TO SAY

Do the best you can until you know better.
Then when you know better, do better.

Maya Angelou

John and I were married for two years before we moved to Europe. We spent three and a half wonderful years in Amsterdam, where we had our two older girls, and traveled extensively. When we returned to Los Angeles, we chose a suburban neighborhood and created a family life together.

One weekend, not too long after we arrived, a group of men that John swam with was getting together for a "men's weekend," so he joined them. The conversation we had when he walked back in the door after the weekend helped our communication from that day forward.

He said that the men in this group really wanted to have good relationships with their wives, and they thought that if their wives would just *tell* them specifically what to do or say, everything would be good. I'm sure it was all said in jest, because we laughed at the seeming ridiculousness of the idea. But in the end, John and I decided to try it out.

Once we began this experiment, I noticed how often I assumed he would know what I wanted him to say or do when he actually had no idea. There were little things, like when I got out of bed first, I really thought that he would know that it was "fair" for him to make the bed and not wait for me to come back in the room. And if I was unloading the dishwasher or putting our laundry away, I really thought he would *know* that I wanted help. Or maybe when I was having an "ugly day" and I would ask him whether an outfit made me look okay, I thought he would know that I didn't really want the truth; I just wanted him to say that he loved me exactly the way I was.

I knew he wasn't a mind reader, but I caught myself wanting him to understand me without my having to be explicit about it. I think I believed that true love was when you knew what the other person was thinking and what they needed in the marriage without having to say it out loud.

At first it was hard for me to ask for what I needed because I soon discovered I wasn't really aware of my own desires. This meant I had to begin to understand what was really going on inside me—what stories I was telling myself and what I wanted. This wasn't as easy as I thought it would be, so expecting John to know was entirely unreasonable. Yet it was also our opportunity to create a new pattern for ourselves.

This new pattern required me to be more clear than I had been in the past, which took some practice. Fortunately, when I asked him directly, John was willing to respond to my requests when he could. He told me that he wanted me to be happy but that he could use a little guidance. "Men are pretty simple," he explained. "We just need instructions."

At times I admit I've taken this strategy to what seems an absurd extreme. I might, in the middle of a conversation, tell him, "This is what I'd like you to say"—and then he'll repeat it back to me exactly. It sounds crazy but he does it in a compassionate and thoughtful way and it makes me feel better. We both laugh about it afterwards and he tells me that he feels better too because he hasn't had to struggle to figure out what to say, and it helps him understand where I'm coming from in that moment.

We agreed to communicate more when we were feeling good instead of waiting until we were frustrated. For example, if I wanted him to help with dinner, kids, homework, banking or anything else, I would *ask* him, rather than just think about it, give him a dirty look or hint that I needed help and wait until he noticed. And he would do the same with me. This took care of frustration on both sides: we both felt more comfortable expressing ourselves, and neither of us had to guess what the other wanted. Today we are each willing to listen to the other's requests—and we're also willing to be vulnerable enough to make them. It's not a perfect system but we're a work in progress. Most importantly we are partners, so we keep trying to get it right.

Many of my clients have similar complaints: their life or business partner isn't helpful when so many things need to get done to make the family or business run smoothly. They want their partner to understand them so well that they can anticipate their needs without anyone having to say anything. However, when the end goal is better communication and more connection, we need to pull out all the tools we have. Sometimes this can be as simple as sharing what you need in the moment with a little more love, compassion and creativity.

—14—

FIXING WHAT ISN'T BROKEN

There is something in every one of you that waits and listens for the sound of the genuine in yourself. It is the only true guide you will ever have. And if you cannot hear it, you will all of your life spend your days on the ends of strings that somebody else pulls.

Howard Thurman

For twenty-five years, whenever John complained about something I'd often offer up a practical solution. I really believed I had the most wonderful ways to solve his problems, whether they concerned his business partner, his commute, his parents, his employees or the traffic.

John listened attentively, but he rarely acted on my recommendations. I couldn't believe this. He seemed to be really struggling, and I kept suggesting all the ways things could get better for him so he could be happy.

John is my husband, my friend, my partner—and I love him dearly. We have raised three remarkable and very different kids. We've dealt with the challenges of sick parents together. We've had different homes, different careers, different friends . . . and we've supported each other through all of it. We really like each other and take care of our relationship. And when we don't "do" parenting or partnering as well as we would like, we forgive each other and try again the next day.

Given all this, I just couldn't figure out why he couldn't see the solutions to his problems the way I did.

In my early coaching days I tried to coach him so he could see that he had a choice. He didn't have to live a life that he didn't like. When things deteriorated at his work and I realized that coaching my partner wasn't a good strategy, my "helpful" suggestions really ramped up. A way out of whatever dilemma he was facing was possible—I just knew it! My only message was that I wanted him to "be happy." We didn't need more things or vacations; we could sell the house and live off that money. John was a free agent and could make his decisions based on what would make him happy.

Not too long ago I was speaking to a coach about my relationship with John. I made an offhand remark about how I couldn't believe that John would choose to continue to struggle with his work.

My coach's question to me was: "Do you think that you're putting a lot of pressure on John to be happy?"

I think I laughed. Was that a thing? Could you put too much pressure on someone to be happy? What is happy anyway?

What I realized in that moment was this: John has always told me how happy he is with his life, but I had never really heard him. He often said he was just sharing with me what was going on at work, for example, and not complaining. It just sounded like complaining to me, a problem in need of a solution. But John assured me that if he wanted to change, he knew he could. More often than not, he really wasn't ready to make a change.

After this conversation with my coach, I asked John if the whole "happy" thing I kept talking about felt like pressure.

He thought about it and agreed—yes, actually, it did. In general, he told me, life was really good. He was just trying to figure out what else was possible for him—in his own way and in his own time.

At that moment I let the whole happy thing go, which was a relief for both of us. Today I love him for exactly who he is, not my version of who I think he should be. When he shares his work life with me now, I hear the issues about traffic, partners and customers differently. We're talking about things that matter to him, and that's what I treasure. I don't have to find any solutions. I can just *be* with him.

I often work with clients who want to help their children, partner or parent when they're complaining about a friend, school or life situation—in the same way I wanted to help John. They are frustrated because the person they're trying to help isn't taking their suggestions. We all want to help people whom we think are suffering, but maybe we're not really seeing what's going on. Maybe they're not looking for a solution; they just want to share what's happening in their life.

John was communicating with me about his life. He didn't want my answers, just a place to process and share what was going on with him. The problem was with me the whole time. I wanted to fix something that was never broken.

— 15 —

BECOMING FLORENCE NIGHTINGALE

Love is our very nature. It's what we are when
we no longer believe our own stories.

Byron Katie

When my sister and I were growing up, both our parents were healthy. They ate well, exercised often, woke up early and had a lot of energy throughout the day. When either of them got sick, it was brief, and it didn't impact my life. They told my sister and me that we were only limited by how well we took care of ourselves and the genes we were given at birth, and we took this to heart. Being sick wasn't a part of the plan.

Looking back, I realize that my mom hid her dark days from us. My sister Kym and I knew that she had experienced a bit of depression when we were young, but our dad had always been there to help, so we didn't really understand what she was going through. In 2007, long after my dad had died, she became severely depressed for the first time. We were surprised, confused, and scared because we didn't have any experience with mental illness. We didn't know yet how debilitating and devastating an illness like depression is.

According to the National Institutes of Mental Health, Major Depressive Disorder ("severe symptoms that interfere with your ability to work, sleep, concentrate, eat and enjoy life") is extremely common in America, affecting more than sixteen million adults according to recent statistics.[1] What is not commonly recognized is how embarrassing and isolating it can be to talk openly about it. At 82, my mom didn't understand this, and neither did we.

The summer she really started deteriorating she was visiting my sister and her family in Boston. Kym and I both recognized something was wrong. When she returned home to Los Angeles, we found that she had lost ten pounds (unintentionally), she wasn't sleeping, she felt isolated and fearful, and she couldn't balance well while walking. I remember her doctors recommending that she use a cane, and Kym and I were both were shocked. It was a dramatic change in my mom's health and although my sister, the doctors and I tried, we couldn't stop her decline. After many tests and doctor visits, a diagnosis of depression, some changes to her medicine routine and an additional twenty pounds of weight loss, we decided to check her in to the psychiatric hospital for help.

They did a great job of caring for her, although every time I visited she begged me to bring her home. After three weeks her weight had stabilized, she seemed calmer and she kept saying how she was REALLY going to be okay if she could just leave, so against the doctor's advice, we acquiesced and took her back to her own home. We had hired full-time help, in addition to

---

[1] "Older Adults and Depression." National Institute of Mental Health. Accessed March 23, 2019. https://www.nimh.nih.gov/health/publications/older-adults-and-depression/index.shtml.

Kym's and my frequent visits, and gave strict instructions on how to keep her upbeat, healthy and eating well. We thought we could "get through it." In retrospect, we were incredibly naïve to think we could help her on our own.

Unfortunately, she started to decline almost immediately, and once again, there was no way to stop it. After four long months at home, she finally agreed to admit herself into the hospital. By that time her depression had deteriorated into a severe psychosis where she refused all medication and interaction with anyone but me and Kym. With our support, the hospital intervened with a longer, more intensive treatment called Electroconvulsive Therapy (ECT). There are a lot of scary stories about ECT—and some wonderful ones as well. Thankfully for my mom, the treatment was transformational. After just a few sessions we had our real mom back. She was in a better place mentally and emotionally than she had been for a long time. It would take her another six months to come back physically, but she had turned a corner thanks to the doctors and ECT.

Now that she was feeling better, something unusual happened: each time I went to see her I found myself feeling sorry for both of us. I hadn't planned to be a "caretaking" type of person. I would get upset about my drive (over an hour each way) or about how I wasn't "supposed" to be taking care of my mother. I'd get agitated and impatient. Then I'd feel guilty for how selfish I was.

Something similar happened with my thinking around taking care of our daughter, Megan. I used to wonder how I ended up in a position where I was taking care of both my aging mother and Megan. Some weeks I found myself at the doctor with my mother several days in a row, and then Megan would get sick and I'd have to cancel my meetings to stay home and look after her.

I know now that any time I get a fixed idea about who I am or what role I'm supposed to play—caretaking daughter, wife, mother—I feel trapped in my story and can't find my way out.

In coaching lingo, that's *victim* language. Feeling sorry for myself—and for my mother and Megan—I would think about what life would look like if I could just focus on *my* agenda, if I could check everything off my to-do list without distraction.

Today I look back and smile, because I know that the only thing that creates sadness and suffering for me—and for everyone in the world—is wanting life to be different than it actually is. I didn't understand that yet. Back then I didn't understand that I had a *choice* in how I saw each of my experiences.

Knowing this has changed my life.

~

This morning I had to cancel a trip to a board meeting I was really looking forward to because Megan is sick and John can't get home in time. But my reaction today was far different from what it would have been in 2007. Rather than thinking that I didn't *want* to stay home to take care of Megan and believing that a change of plans is a bad thing, I immediately started thinking about where the opportunity was in this.

So many wonderful things came to mind that I could do with a full day at home loving and taking care of Megan, including writing this chapter. I was filled with a deep sense of gratitude that I have the flexibility to be able to change my plans and understand that either option—the meeting or staying home with Megan—was great.

Since hiring my first coach, I have spent time reading books, listening to audios, meditating, and conversing with many coaches to deeply understand the truth that WE create our own suffering and disappointment, or well-being and joy, through our *thinking* about a circumstance. It's not the circumstance that creates our feelings. The story I'd held on to—that against my will I'd become Florence Nightingale, the founder of modern nursing—didn't have to be my truth any longer.

Today, I know that I have *chosen* to help John, our girls, my mom, my clients and the world at large . . . and I am filled with gratitude that this is how I now see the world.

Of course, it's possible I will get impatient the next time something similar happens—but once I remember that it's my thinking and my choice, I can relax and choose something else.

Coaching has helped me see that I have a choice in every circumstance, and every circumstance offers its own unique possibilities. Any long drive, like the one I used to make to the hospital, is a possibility to learn something new from an audiobook or podcast—so the drive hasn't changed, just the opportunity I see with the drive.

Something my clients hear me say often is that a happy and full life is not only how you live the good, comfortable and smooth times, it's also how you choose to live the inevitable bumpy, scary, confusing, heartbreaking times. This means that I can always ask "Where's the opportunity?" no matter the circumstance. When we can see our situations through a different lens, our mind and heart feel lighter.

My mom is still alive at ninety-three and the doctors, Kym and I continue to help her manage her depression, which reappears at times. Looking back, there have been many opportunities that have grown out of my mom's illness. Possibly the greatest gift of the whole experience was that my sister and I transformed our relationship. We became each other's partner and friend in a way that we hadn't been before, and I am deeply grateful for that.

ON
PARENTING

— 16 —

WHY I STARTED MEDITATING

Meditation is not a way of making your mind quiet. It is a way of entering into the quiet that is already there - buried under the 50,000 thoughts the average person thinks every day.

~ Deepak Chopra

Our third daughter, Megan, was born in March, 1999. We were, of course, overjoyed, and at first everything in our lives seemed to be going along a relatively normal path (as much as that's possible with three kids—it was a very full life). Then, around the time Megan turned one, we started noticing that she was sensitive to crowds and loud noises. Up until that point we thought she was just a calmer child, but we soon realized that she was also slower to reach growth milestones. When she was two and couldn't express herself as well as most of her peers, we knew something was different.

During those first few years, Megan was sweet and loving, but she cried constantly. As a result, I was on edge with everyone. The habits I had so carefully cultivated to center myself were no longer enough to enable an even-tempered conversation in the evenings. It was as though my patience had a time limit. When it was homework time for the big girls, I was tired and I would get upset at the smallest things. I'd yell and sometimes even cry, to the point where I didn't recognize myself. My family understood when I broke down. Everyone in our house bore some of the stress. But I hated feeling so exhausted, frustrated and emotional, and it made me sad that I couldn't help Megan more.

Eventually I decided that if I didn't find a new way to cope, I would stay stuck in my current pattern, which was unsustainable. I felt desperate. About this time, Michelle, a friend who was studying Buddhism, introduced me to her meditation practice.

Before I started meditating regularly, I was convinced that there was no way I could sit still that long. For years I had been curious about the process but completely intimidated by trying to figure out the "real" way to meditate. I had convinced myself that there were too many obstacles to overcome because of my personality and life circumstances, so I never tried.

I've always had a lot of energy. These days I wake up early and work on many different projects at a time. Every day feels like an opportunity, and I don't want to miss a minute of it. On the other hand, this energy hasn't always been positive. In fact, I sometimes felt overwhelmed or stressed because I had so much energy. To make matters worse, I occasionally came on too strong with other people, and they didn't like it. And from my perspective it felt like I was constantly "managing" my energy.

So I developed ways to calm myself down, creating habits that I still have in place today: regular exercise, eating healthy foods, getting enough sleep and not drinking too much alcohol.

This daily routine still supports my mental, physical and emotional health and helps me stay centered. But until I was almost forty, my daily routine didn't include a spiritual practice because I didn't understand the incredible benefits of one.

After Megan was born, I hit a major bump in my path and wasn't sure what to do. My normal means of relaxing and re-centering no longer seemed up to the new challenges that I was dealing with. I now know that the bumps in our paths are chances to grow, so I actively look for these opportunities in every situation. Fortunately, even then, I used my stress and frustration as the push I needed to try meditation in earnest.

It changed my life.

Michelle explained that meditation, along with being an opportunity to be kind and gentle with myself, is about living in the moment. She suggested that one way for me to do this was to simply focus on my breath going in and out of my nostrils for a few minutes a day. Every time I thought about something other than my breath, all I had to do was gently remind myself to come back to the sensation of air going in and out of my nose. She explained that having thoughts appear as you meditate is a completely normal part of the practice. Thoughts are like clouds in the sky, and if you notice them passing by, you just go back to the breath without judgement.

I did a few sessions together with Michelle. Thankfully she knew me well, so when I became fidgety, she would ask if I wanted a break—even if it was only after a few minutes. She never made me feel that meditation was a very serious or somber endeavor, only that it was an experiment. We also talked about the fact that it's called a meditation "practice" for a reason: with more time it becomes easier to sit and focus for longer stretches.

For my first day of solo meditation I woke up early so that I was the only one awake. I sat outside looking at a small rock a friend had given me, and I timed myself—starting with five minutes felt manageable. I stared intensely at the rock, looking at all the colors and bumps, feeling the air going in and out of my nose, and listening to my breath. Whenever a random thought showed up, like the thought of needing to pay a bill, I reminded myself to return my attention to the rock and the sensation and sound of my breath. It felt silly to be looking at a rock, but I needed a visual distraction because closing my eyes didn't work at first. When I closed my eyes, my thoughts started racing, and it was a struggle to focus on my breath, so I did what Michelle said and made it easy for myself.

For one month, a few days a week, I sat for five minutes at a time. If I wanted to go longer, I let myself, but five minutes was what I had committed to. At that point in my life I felt exhausted most of the time, but I told myself I didn't have to wake up much earlier for only five minutes of meditation.

As it turned out, breathing and looking at a rock or a leaf or a flower made me feel better, and I was inspired to keep going. I was excited to have time away from all the busyness of life, the constant worrying, the excessive planning and the nagging feeling that I wasn't good enough. As I meditated, I discovered a more peaceful voice inside me, one that had been buried beneath the chaos of everyday life. I knew one thing for certain: *I wanted more of that voice in my life.*

When I shared my progress with Michelle, she gently told me that five minutes was a great beginning, but if I could do it, twenty minutes was better. My first thought was that this was too much for me to commit to. But on reflection I realized that I was still getting upset with the kids and John on a regular basis. Although I felt better, all the initial issues that "drove" me to meditation in the first place were still hanging around. More to the point, I still didn't feel like the best version of me. So, I made a commitment to myself to meditate for twenty minutes, three times a week, over a three-month period, and then to evaluate what my next steps would be.

What I ultimately found was that meditation helped me "do life" more smoothly. I felt better, calmer, more relaxed, happier—and I laughed more. The small things didn't trigger me the way they used to.

If I needed further proof, I realized that if I missed my meditation practice too many days in a row, it wasn't just me who noticed. For example, I thought everything was going smoothly until one day when I pushed the kids a bit too hard to get out of the house for school. Megan started slowing (and breaking) down, which made the whole family late, and I lost my cool.

Later that evening when John and I were dissecting what had gone wrong that morning, he asked me how long it had been since I'd meditated. I told him it had been a few days, and in that moment realized that it wasn't just about me—the entire family was benefitting from the changes my meditation practice was bringing about in me.

It's been more than seventeen years since that transformational day when I was desperate enough to give meditation a serious try. Early on it was hard for me to find the time to meditate, and just sitting still was a challenge. Today it's a wonderful and important part of my day, every day. I went from meditating a few days a week to meditating at least once a day for a minimum of twenty minutes. Most mornings these days, it's actually thirty to sixty minutes—and the time flies by. That quiet hour or so before the house wakes up is still my favorite time of day, and it's also become the time when John and I meditate together.

~

I tried meditation because I was desperate. But you don't have to wait. These days there are countless studies out there showing the benefits of meditation. Here are two interesting findings:

- Harvard researcher Sara Lazar and her team discovered that a regular meditation practice is likely to positively impact areas of the brain related to decision-making and focus, as well as to reduce stress.[2]

- Richard Davidson, professor of psychology at the University of Wisconsin–Madison, points out that "If you go back to the 1950s, the majority of middle-class citizens in Western countries did not regularly engage in physical exercise. It was because of scientific research that established the importance of physical exercise in promoting health and well-being that more people now engage in regular physical exercise. I think mental exercise will be regarded in a similar way 20 years from now." Meditation is the exercise for your brain.[3]

---

[2] Learn more about her research at https://scholar.harvard.edu/sara_lazar/home
[3] Tenenbaum, David. "Changing Brains for the Better; Article Documents Benefits of Multiple Practices." University of Wisconsin-Madison News. April 17, 2012. Accessed April 17, 2019. https://news.wisc.edu/changing-brains-for-the-better-article-documents-benefits-of-multiple-practices/

I've shared all this because I want to point out that—as the saying goes—if *I* can do this, *anyone* can do this. It was very helpful to me at the beginning to realize that there is no perfect way to meditate. You can do it anywhere, it doesn't cost any money and the rewards are *huge* if you stay with it. And another reason they call it a meditation "practice" is because it takes practice to settle your mind. There's no pressure to get it "right," and you don't have to be desperate to "make it happen." I've taken classes, read books and talked to many people about meditation over the years. There's lots of information out there. But in the end, it's simply about getting started, experimenting with it—for a few weeks or months or years, and seeing how it makes you feel.

— 17 —

THE BEAUTY OF SINGING

The only thing better than singing is more singing.

Ella Fitzgerald

Megan is eighteen and sings all the time. She has loved to sing since she was little. When she speaks, her speech is stilted and slow, but when she sings, it's fluid. She relaxes into the music and it just flows out of her.

Until recently I wasn't able to see the pure joy that she feels when she sings. Megan performed acapella at the talent shows in her elementary and middle schools. Her sisters, John and I used to go to her performances, and at first we would cringe. In fact, we would all want to hide when people said how proud of her they were. She has a beautiful voice, but we were embarrassed because either she didn't sing the correct words, she was off tune or she sang the song more slowly than how we thought it should be.

Megan didn't care at all. She sang her heart out and people loved her for who she was. In third grade, all she talked about was Adele. For the talent show that year, she sang Adele's

"Chasing Pavements" all alone on stage—just her and a single microphone. She had spent hours practicing around the house, singing in the shower, on the couch, at the dinner table—so she would have it perfect when it was her time to perform. Except that each time she sang the song, she sang "chasing *payments*" instead of "chasing *pavements*."

Our family was determined to help her see that she needed to sing the correct words. So we showed her the actual lyrics. We made her watch the video a number of times (in which Adele walks on the sidewalk and people are dancing on the pavement all around her). In the middle of the song we interrupted her and wrote the *correct* words on cards for her.

She absolutely refused to change what she wanted to sing.

So what happened? The performance was a big success and she was *so* proud of herself. We were so proud of her too.

Today I reflect back on how many times I've tried to change someone's mind using tactics of rational thinking, convinced that I knew the "right" way to do something. I've already written about how often people just want to be listened to and not have someone "solve" their problems for them. It's also true that people want to make decisions on their own, and this makes perfect sense. In Megan's case, the reason we wanted her to sing the words the way Adele sang them was so she wouldn't embarrass herself in front of the audience. What I failed to understand then was that *she* wasn't embarrassed; she was just excited to sing. *We* were embarrassed that she wasn't doing it "correctly."

Many years have passed since those days and I have a new appreciation of Megan's singing and her bravery. She never had the same fear of embarrassing herself that I did. Today she sings soprano in the high school choir. She spends hours singing all day and into the evening at home. She sings to friends on the phone and to guests who come over. She sings when she's getting her hair cut, when she's in the grocery store and when she's walking the dog. People look at her because it's an unusual thing to do. She doesn't mind, or maybe she doesn't notice.

I have no idea if she's singing the songs correctly, but I no longer worry about it like I once did. I see her singing and feel the pure, unfiltered love of life that comes from her.

It doesn't get better than that. When we don't hold ourselves back, we experience our invisible connection to universal energy and creativity.

— 18 —

Who We See

*Through compassion, you find that all
human beings are just like you.*

Dalai Lama

Growing up in my house, everyone had labels. I know today that they *are* labels, but at the time I didn't know there was such a thing; people were just who they were as described by my parents.

A label is defined as "a descriptive or identifying word or phrase."[4] We see people through the lens of the labels we've given them, and we rationalize their decisions and actions based on their labels. In the lingo of my family, people were smart, happy, angry, fat, pretty, athletic, lazy, a "stupe" (someone who was stupid in my dad's eyes), or "sharp" (by which I think my dad meant quick-witted). As the oldest child, one of my labels was "responsible and capable . . . with potential." One of my sister's labels was "she needs extra help because school doesn't

---

[4] "Label." Merriam-Webster. Accessed March 23, 2019.
https://www.merriam-webster.com/dictionary/label.

come easily." I never questioned these labels, and I grew up believing that people don't change. In fact, many people say just that, almost like a mantra: "People don't change."

But people DO change. My parents were wrong. I have changed and have witnessed real change with my clients. Labels trap us, keep us locked into one way of being. We begin to believe what they say about us, and then our actions are based on those beliefs.

Both my mom and dad enjoyed watching people. In the 70s, our family would go to the airport early to observe all the people on their way to or from somewhere. As we waited, we created elaborate stories based on what the people looked like. It was imaginative and fun because our stories were about where they were going, what job they had and who they were outside of the airport. We talked about their physical features, their voices and accents, and how tall or short or old or young they were. We talked about hair and skin color, the clothes they wore, and the bags they carried. It was a game to be as creative as we could be with our stories, and people transformed before our eyes.

I thought that was normal—to identify people just by how they acted, what they looked like or what job they had—until I had a conversation with Megan a little while ago. Although Megan was described as having special needs from the time she was three, it was becoming apparent to me that she also had special *powers*: of non-judgment, compassion and acceptance.

Each year Megan has an aide at school who helps her with taking notes, doing classwork and simplifying complicated topics. In preschool and elementary school, I always knew the wonderful women who were with Megan throughout the day. In middle school, she joined a special day class and no longer had an aide, but she returned to one-on-one support in high school. One year in high school, Megan had the same aide as the previous year. A few weeks into the school year, Megan and I were talking in the car and I asked her what Ms. B looked like, because I was trying to find her at open house. The conversation went something like this.

Me: Megan, what does Ms. B. look like?

Megan: I don't know.

Me: What?

Megan: I don't know what you mean.

Me: I mean what color hair does she have? Blond? Brown? Very Dark? Like mine?

Megan: I can't remember.

Me: How tall she is? My height? Shorter than you? Taller?

Megan: I can't remember.

Me: I'm confused sweetie, how can you not remember what the woman who has been working with you for two years looks like?

I kept this up for a bit longer until I realized that she *really doesn't see somebody's outside.* After even more questions it was clear she couldn't remember Ms. B's hair or skin color.

It was absolutely wonderful to witness. It's not something she's practiced or decided to change; it's who she is. Megan doesn't see someone as good or bad either. She sees people doing things that aren't nice to another person and she doesn't like it, but she doesn't call the *person* bad. She doesn't say someone is kind either. "Bad" and "kind" are both labels, and she doesn't see the world like that.

We're not stuck with labels either, whether we've given them to ourselves or someone else has applied them to us. *Choosing* what we see in another person, and in ourselves, is empowering. We have the power to change who we are and how we see the world, and when we play with our perspectives, we can see something *new*.

What labels have you put on yourself or someone else that you want to change?

~

P. S. My sister didn't let her label stop her even though it was true that school wasn't easy. Today I'm proud to say that she has two master's degrees and is a public health professor at a university in Boston.

— 19 —

CLIMBING ADVENTURES

This is not how your story ends.
It's simply where it takes a turn you didn't expect.

Cheryl Strayed

Our girls grew up appreciating the outdoors, clean air, running streams, camping and travel without the comforts of home. John and I had both spent time backpacking when we were young—and we still love it today—so we wanted our girls to share our sense of adventure and curiosity about the environment.

This included rock climbing. When the girls were three, six and eight we started bringing them to a rock climbing gym to play around and get exercise. This was a gym where you could take lessons and learn the basics before venturing outside.

Our middle daughter, Lauren, was a particularly active toddler. She escaped her crib at nine months old and quickly took to walking everywhere and climbing on the furniture. When she was three years old we brought her to preschool and she immediately proceeded to climb their biggest tree, at which point the directors put a rope around the tree limiting how high kids could climb. In other words, climbing was in her blood early on, so when her cousins were staying with us in Los Angeles, we decided that it would be fun for the older girls to do a rock climbing class together. (They had already spent some time at a rock-climbing camp that summer.) So one day my sister and I dropped them off and went about our own day together.

The next thing I knew I received a panicked call from my sister: her daughter Amelia had fallen onto her back from the top of the rock-climbing wall (which was about twenty feet high).

My sister raced to the gym and took Amelia to the hospital along with the girls. I arrived a few minutes after them to find that my niece was doing okay—but Lauren was in shock.

Lauren and Amelia had been taking turns climbing the wall. Somewhere along the way they both forgot to check that Amelia was clipped into the rope on her way up. When it came time for her to rappel down, she didn't have her safety latch on—and she did a free fall from the top of the rock to the mat below, landing on her back. Lauren told me that she heard the air go out of Amelia's lungs and was so scared that she was frozen stiff. She literally couldn't move.

We were incredibly fortunate. Amelia was okay—only a sore back and hip that lingered for a little while. It obviously could have been much worse.

But Lauren couldn't forgive herself. She felt she hadn't moved quickly enough and that she wasn't there to help someone she loved so much in a time of need. In the days and months that followed she couldn't stop thinking about what happened. In fact, for over a year she would wake up from a recurring nightmare in which she couldn't help someone in trouble when they really needed her.

And the memory kept repeating itself when she was awake as well. She had frozen when she wished she had taken action The same scene played out over and over in her head, constantly reinforcing in her mind that she didn't have the voice or the skills she needed when she desperately wanted to help her cousin. She stopped having sleepovers with her friends because she was scared she'd have a bad dream, and she would come home after school worried about different things that had never bothered her before.

We tried to help at home. John and I spent time talking to Lauren about all the reasons why her reaction was perfectly normal. We strategized on what to do if it ever happened again and read books about how to help in a crisis situation. Amelia also kept telling Lauren that everything was okay, that she wasn't upset or hurt. This "logical" input from all of us helped a little, but Lauren couldn't shake the feeling that she would do the same thing again. Her fear was undermining her sense of confidence and trust in herself.

Then one day something clicked and all of the conversations we'd been having made sense. After that, Lauren resolved to take action.

Together we strategized on how she could use her experience to guide her future choices and make decisions from a place of power rather than fear. The last thing she wanted was to stay scared, constantly asking: "What happens next time?"

Lauren began building the skills she needed to help people in times of need. She started with Junior Lifeguards at the beach, where she learned CPR and lifesaving techniques. She worked as a swim instructor and lifeguard and became a certified rescue scuba diver. Equally important, she learned to keep a level head in times of crisis. Over the years, every time she has had to make hard decisions about who to call and how to help in times of emergency, she has done so from a place of confidence born of practice.

Lauren very methodically chose small ways to empower herself. She has shown me how to build on challenging experiences rather than hide from them. Today she works at REI, an outdoor-gear retail store, and she just started rock climbing again for the first time since her cousin's fall.

It takes courage to stop living from a place of fear. But it's always that first small step towards intentional growth that opens the door to the incredible power within us. When I work with my clients, we talk about past experiences that have had a negative impact on them, and we often come up with ways to use those moments as turning points for positive change.

Lauren decided her fear wouldn't limit her choices in life. We can all make the same decision and use our experiences to propel us forward.

A LEARNING OPPORTUNITY

Between stimulus and response there is a space. In that space is our power to choose our response. In our response lies our growth and our freedom.

Victor Frankl

Many years ago we were on a family vacation with some close friends and one of the parents criticized my parenting of Megan. The kids were playing in the living room while we parents milled around getting ready for the whole group of us to go out to dinner. Megan, who was lying on the ground, grabbed her older sister's foot as she walked by. I'm not sure Megan knew what would happen next, but Murphy—who turned twelve years old that day—fell to the ground with a thud and stood up furious.

Hearing the anger, I walked into the living room and chose for the moment to let them work it out without interference from me. Murphy retaliated by sitting on Megan's stomach. Megan soon started crying, at which point I split the two up, talked to her older sister first about how she could have responded differently, then spoke to Megan about not grabbing feet because it's dangerous for the other person.

I thought I handled it pretty well. Both kids were upset but recovering, and nobody was hurt. It was at this point that the other parent went over to Megan, picked her up and told me that I wasn't protecting Megan well enough in our family. She went on to emotionally explain to everyone in the room that Megan wasn't able to defend herself and that my attention was misplaced by speaking to our older daughter first.

Was she right? Did I blow it? I felt angry and defensive because I knew she had absolutely no idea what it was like to parent Megan. I kept thinking that it would have been so much better if she had pulled me aside and had a real conversation about what she witnessed, instead of sharing her thoughts in front of all the kids. I felt betrayed by a good friend and upset with her for thinking she knew more than I did in this situation.

Yet at the same time I felt guilty and embarrassed. I asked myself if she was correct in her assessment of the situation, and after hearing her out I realized that she was right: I should have made sure Megan was okay before focusing on Murphy.

If I'm honest with myself, I acted without thinking when I went to Murphy first. I told myself that I was trying to do what I thought was best based on many experiences with my daughters, but I was reacting to a completely frustrating situation without thinking through my response. To make matters worse, the confrontation made me question for the hundredth time if I was the best mom for Megan and Murphy.

In short, it was a bad situation, and our fun evening turned into an uncomfortable dinner. Ultimately, we went home early from vacation, with me still wondering what I could have done differently.

Megan is slow and cautious, which is hard when you're traveling with people who don't know her routine. She wakes up, eats, walks, talks and processes information more slowly than her typical peers, and when we're trying to get out of the house, she seems to move even slower.

Because of this, and because Megan is such a loving person, people want to protect her from the outside world. As her family, we too want to protect her. Many times it's hard not to simply solve for her whatever immediate problem she's facing instead of allowing her the space to figure things out for herself. As her parents, we try to remember that she needs to develop skills and resilience to be able to grow into her potential, so we try to make decisions from that place.

As I continued to think about what happened on our vacation, it finally dawned on me that there would be no way for this other family to know any of this, much less how to really communicate with Megan. Why not? *Because we'd never told them.* I had assumed they would figure it out on their own because we had been on vacations together before. But in this particular instance, it made perfect sense for the other parent to want to protect Megan from her sister Murphy, who is five years older. From her perspective it could have seemed like I wasn't doing enough.

It shocked me to realize that I had never thought of talking to people about Megan's challenges directly. At that time, we didn't have a diagnosis or know the reason behind her processing delay, but today we know that she's missing a piece of a chromosome. Our thinking was that we didn't want to put a label on her and potentially limit her growth, so we didn't talk about how she was different from her typical peers. We also didn't consider how to help other people understand her better. Our decisions around these issues were made from a place of innocence, but it was clearly time to reassess and make some changes.

Thankfully, our family all agreed that this was our opportunity to take action. The first thing we did was to begin meeting with a therapist. Our agenda was to learn how to talk to Megan about how she learns differently from some of her friends, and then to develop ways to communicate with other people about her learning disabilities.

At home we really believed that we weren't treating Megan that much like a "special" kid. However, when we finally talked about it with the therapist, we saw we were mistaken in that assessment. Our expectations of Megan were very different. We attempted to have her do small chores but didn't worry if they didn't get done. We had charts and checklists so she could become more independent—for example, specific morning and evening routines—but when she wasn't able to do them we stepped in. I carried her in a backpack much of the day, even when she could walk comfortably herself.

We also realized that we had become desensitized to her crying because it felt like she cried all the time. This of course wasn't true—she smiled and hugged and loved on us often as well. But when she *did* cry there were many rational reasons for it. For one thing, she found it challenging and frustrating to communicate well. She couldn't process conversations as quickly as she needed to, so she became confused and couldn't participate. When there was too much loud noise or too many people around she experienced a kind of sensory overload. All of these issues and others brought tears, and this made perfect sense.

In those early days we found we couldn't always figure out

what was wrong and what her crying meant, and we didn't know if we really needed to be worried about something or not. Sometimes it was just easier to pick her up or solve a problem for her to help her through her tears.

So despite how hard we tried, we definitely didn't treat her the same as our other kids. With the therapist's help we were finally able to take a look at how that impacted all of us, including Megan. Parenting is not a straightforward process with typical kids, and it's even less clear with a child who has special needs. This was our chance to learn how to work as a team to get better.

When Megan's older sister sat on her, I didn't respond to her crying in the way my friend expected me to because to me this was a familiar situation. Temporarily tuning out the crying helped us make it through tough days when Megan was younger, but it was no longer the right strategy. Instead we decided to take responsibility for our communication with Megan, and for helping other people interact successfully with her.

As it turned out, that awkward interaction with our friend was an incredible gift. Today, we know how to describe who Megan is and how to best communicate with her. What's more, at nineteen she can now tell people herself. Understanding this, she is now also taking greater responsibility for her communication with other people. For example, she can now tell someone "just a minute" or "let me think about that" before responding, and people are willing to wait.

That conversation was a huge turning point for all of us.

The next time we traveled with this same family, we sat down with them and described our parenting approach, how our girls interact with each other, and how best to connect with

Megan. The holiday went much more smoothly because our friends had more information and an open space in which to ask questions—and because we were now a family that was finally relaxed and not trying to keep up appearances.

~

When one of my clients asked me the other day how I would feel if someone made a comment critical of my parenting, I had this experience at the ready. She was in the midst of considering a strategy with her own special-needs child that might have looked unconventional to anybody watching. But of course you don't need to have a special child to elicit well-meaning comments from family, friends or strangers on how you raise your kids. People start giving advice when you're pregnant and they continue to want to help no matter how old your child is.

I've learned that the comments usually come from a good and helpful place—the other person wants to help when they think they see a problem, so they innocently suggest something that worked for them or that would bring relief to an uncomfortable situation. And yet it's often hard to take such comments in this spirit. It hurts so much if someone criticizes our parenting because it's really the one thing we don't want to get wrong.

Consequently, it's almost impossible for any of us to see the value in what someone says when you hear it as criticism. It's even harder when you begin to think that they may be right and you start questioning your actions.

I had the opportunity to choose how I reacted to our friend's comments. It took me a while, but our decision to use it as a learning opportunity for our family gave us an additional opportunity to receive unintended benefits. Rather than closing off that relationship, we opened up our communication between ourselves and our friends, and in the process developed tools that all of us use to this day.

— 21 —

UNINTENDED BENEFITS

You cannot hope to build a better world without improving the individuals. To that end, each of us must work for his own improvement and, at the same time, share a general responsibility for all humanity, our particular duty being to aid those to whom we think we can be most useful.

Marie Curie

We had gone to the therapist to help us become better communicators with and about Megan, but something else unexpectedly emerged from our sessions

Our middle daughter, Lauren, is the kind of person who naturally wants to help people. She listens compassionately and accepts people for who they are. She has an amazing laugh and you immediately feel like you can talk to and count on her. Because Megan felt this too, John and I used it to our advantage.

Megan calmed down when Lauren talked to her, so when we were at our wits' end and she had shut down on John and me completely, we turned to Lauren for help. She would climb into bed and snuggle with Megan or sit with her on the couch when she was crying, angry or sad. Lauren didn't even have to say anything; her presence was enough to help Megan shift. Then, once Megan had settled down, Lauren could hand her back to us and we would take over.

As part of our family therapy, each of us had separate conversations about what was going on in our lives. Lauren shared with the therapist that she was feeling a lot of stress when I went out of town for work because she felt responsible for Megan when I was gone. When her dad was having a hard time with Megan, he would often ask Lauren for help, not knowing that Lauren was feeling that kind of pressure. I didn't know it either. And it was typically in the evening when John and I were just focused on doing anything we could to get her to bed.

At about the same time, I began noticing that Lauren had created strict before-bed routines for herself. We would have to kiss her a certain number of times after we read a book or close the door and turn off the light a certain way and then lie with her for a specific amount of time. These were small things, but they went on long enough for me to notice the pattern, so I brought them up to the therapist myself.

Because it was now out in the open, we could talk about it together as a family. John and I were able to see that we needed to stop relying on Lauren when it got hard with Megan. Lauren also began to recognize that she was taking too much responsibility for Megan's wellbeing even when we didn't ask, and to see that this was having stressful effects on her. I'm not sure we would have been able to work through this had we not been working with a therapist who knew us all.

As a consequence of these sessions, Lauren gradually reduced the routines she needed before bed. I remember her imagining clouds in the sky with just one letter on each cloud: C. A. L. M. She would say the letters separately and then the whole word to herself, and when she focused on calm and the clouds, she could settle herself down and fall asleep without the routines she had clung to. These calming, meditative techniques helped her relax in a way that she hadn't been able to before.

Maybe, I thought at the time, the *real* invisible reason we went to the therapist was to help Lauren. Sometimes we think we do something for one reason, and another powerful, unintended benefit appears.

— 22 —

THE VON QUINN FAMILY SINGERS

We don't sing because we're happy,
we're happy because we sing.

William James

When our kids were little, someone told me that we should sing to them. When I protested that I didn't have a good voice, she told me the kids wouldn't care. She explained that the feelings of love and joy were all that would matter to them. So we began to sing without the fear of being judged. Thinking back now, that advice, which allowed us to see the situation differently, gave us the freedom to sing whatever we wanted without worry.

It was easy to sing to our babies. Just the soothing sound of our voices brought them peace and calm and lulled them to sleep. We didn't believe that our beautiful babies would be laughing or judging us when we inevitably sang off key, chose the wrong words or stopped in the middle of a song.

That wasn't true, however, as the kids got older. They gradually became more aware of other people and noticed the difference between things they liked and things they didn't like as much. And sometimes they seemed to feel self-conscious about *everything* John and I did. By that time however, we had already started singing before bed each night, so they were used to the routine, and our singing didn't seem to embarrass them.

When the kids were little, I made up a soothing song based on a familiar tune ("Lullaby and Good Night") and added their names and silly things they did in the day to the song. As they got older, we sang songs I remembered from my own childhood—like "Raindrops on Roses" and "Doe a Deer" from *The Sound of Music*—or newer ones like "Christopher Robin" by Kenny Loggins, "Circle Game" by Joni Mitchell and "Leaving on a Jet Plane" by Peter, Paul & Mary. Every night we would go into their room, tuck them into bed, read a book and sing a few songs. It was our nighttime ritual, and after a while, the girls knew the songs by heart.

Occasionally I would ask babysitters if they would be willing to sing the girls a song as a bedtime treat. Each young woman laughed and explained they didn't know how to sing and it would be too embarrassing, so they didn't think they could do it. And each time I shared that the girls weren't going to judge their singing—they just loved to hear someone sing before they went to bed. What's more, Megan wasn't going to be able to go to sleep easily without a song. They would finally agree and admit to us later that it was fun to sing with the girls.

All three girls slept in the same room until they were ten. As they got older they slept in different but adjoining rooms and John and I would sit in the hallway to sing so they could each hear the songs. John had been shy about his guitar playing since he didn't consider himself to be as good as he wanted to be, but like the singing, the girls didn't care, and in fact were thrilled to have him play.

Eventually he played whatever songs he could find in his old guitar books and we tried out new songs together. Megan especially loved the songs before bed and held on to the tradition until she was much older. For her I made up a special song that included what she was going to do the next day.

Singing is therapy for Megan. When she sings, she's relaxed and happy, much like she was when I would sing to her before bed. It's hard for her to speak and process information quickly, but when she sings it's different; it flows from her and lights her up.

Singing does that to people—it lights us all up. Even though we didn't think we had very good voices, John and I had the good fortune to sing with our kids, and as it turned out they didn't care whether or not we could sing everything in tune. When they had sleepovers, I sang to their friends as well. Our nieces and nephews remember me singing when they came for holidays or summer vacation.

I recently asked Murphy, our oldest daughter, whether she remembered any of the words to the songs I used to sing. At first she said no, but when I began to sing she found she could sing along beautifully. She was shocked that she remembered all the words, and the experience brought back her childhood memories of lying in bed while we sang to her, and of her sometimes joining in.

As I reflect on those evenings when we didn't think we had enough time, and the kids were getting to bed later than we wanted, and the homework wasn't fully complete, I'm happy that John and I didn't let our own judgements about ourselves hold us back from creating this wonderful connection with our girls.

Singing makes people feel good. It brings our energy up and it connects our hearts together with an invisible string. Singing has brought more love, laughter and silliness into our home because we didn't worry about being judged and we didn't take ourselves or our singing too seriously.

Makes me wonder: what else would I do if I didn't think people were judging me?

— 23 —

Taking Responsibility

Even when there is no other cause for inattention, men are more prone to neglect their duty when they think that another is attending to it.

Aristotle

Because I was so involved in our local schools, our kids frequently heard stories I brought home from the parent meetings. In fact, I sometimes shared details at the dinner table that weren't always easy to hear because the stories were from parents with kids in kindergarten through twelfth grade (from five to eighteen years old), and ours were still in elementary school at the time.

I remember one meeting when the president of the high-school Parent Teacher Association (PTA) told us about something I'd never heard of before: cutting. Today I know that cutting is when people cut or scratch themselves somewhere on their body so it bleeds. The opinion of professionals at the time was that this was a call for help from these young people.

That night I shared about cutting at the dinner table. I explained that this was someone asking for help by their actions instead of their words, and we agreed that if anyone were to see this at school, she was to go immediately to the school counselor, because they would be able to help. We talked about feeling compassion for the person who was cutting themselves, and about recognizing that it was a call for help in the only way they knew how. By getting them help, we would be doing what we could—and what was best for the person—and from there, the professionals could take over.

Shortly thereafter, Murphy started sixth grade at a new middle school. One day within the first few months, she came home crying hysterically. Once she settled down, she told us that she had seen a girl at a locker near hers with blood dripping down her leg and the word "death" scratched into her leg. She knew the right thing to do was to go to the counselor and talk to her about it, but it felt *really* hard to do that, so she came home to talk to us about it first. She was convinced that if people found out about her going to a counselor for something like this, she would be forever banned from all the middle school friend groups.

John and I sat down with Murphy to strategize a plan of action that would help this young girl and still respect what was important to Murphy. Murphy knew that the most critical thing was to help this individual, so we ultimately decided that early the next morning, before school started, we would go and talk to the counselor together.

Fortunately the counselor was brilliant and took over quickly, explaining to all of us that she would take good care of this young girl. She also assured Murphy that in middle school, things pass quickly on to the next social crisis, and that it was likely nobody would know of Murphy's involvement. She told us that she would contact this girl's parents and they would get her the help she needed—and that's exactly what happened.

Sometimes doing what you know is best is different and much harder than doing the socially acceptable or easy thing. This is not just true when you're in middle school but throughout our lives. It can be easy to pretend that you don't see or hear something and just walk by, and it's easy not take action, thinking (hoping) that someone else will take care of it.

However, when we remember that we are all connected to each other by an invisible thread of light and love, and we slow it down for ourselves to look at the ripple effects of our choices, it's easier to make a clear decision and take action for the greater good of all. As parents, one of the gifts we can give our kids is to help them think deeply, to look at various aspects of a situation and to allow *them* to come to a good decision for everyone involved. It's much better than having us hand them our "correct" answer. This way when they're not with us, they will have experience making those decisions on their own.

— 24 —

GROUNDHOG DAY

I've got to admit it's getting better
A little better all the time

John Lennon & Paul McCartney

Groundhog Day with Bill Murray and Andie MacDowell is one of my favorite movies of all time. It's about how Phil Connors goes from being his worst self as a sarcastic and cynical news reporter to a much better version of himself when he gets caught in a kind of time loop and is forced to repeat the same day over and over until he gets it right. It's fun to watch because sometimes I want to do the same thing myself. Some days, all I want is the opportunity to do my day over again—and do it better the second time.

For many years, the way I recovered at the end of the day was to think over all the conversations I'd had and decide what I would say if I could have a "do-over." Occasionally, if there was something I'd said to a friend or family member that I could have said in a better way, I would call and ask if I could say whatever it was over again, differently. When email became an option, I would send a follow-up email explaining in great detail what my real intention was and that my original words likely did not reflect that.

Most times people would respond with surprise because they didn't know what I was talking about. They would laugh and I would laugh, and I would feel better that my clearer, wiser self could show up.

I often had this same wish—to repeat the same day over, just better—when I became a parent. Many times, I would get upset with one of the kids, and after we had all settled down I would think of alternative responses I could have had to the interaction. Those different responses might have led to the same outcome; that is, whatever decision I made as a parent might have ended up the same. But I imagined that they would have left both of us feeling better about it.

With the kids, however, I couldn't send them an email or call them with a conversational re-do like I could with my friends, although I tried many times. If we'd had an argument before bedtime, I would go to their bedroom and inevitably find a sign on the door saying "NO MOMS" or "Keep out." I did it enough times with the girls that they started to tell me that they knew I would be back to apologize and that it was all okay. If we'd had an argument about curfew or cleaning up their room, I would occasionally go back later and say whatever I had said but "better." I desperately wanted to be okay with whatever I said in the moment so I wouldn't have to think about the conversation again.

When John and I started making a joke about our foibles as parents, much of the emotion behind trying to get it perfect shifted.

One night after dinner and homework and some tears, I looked at John and said, "Wow, I could have done that parenting thing better." He smiled and agreed, and then we started laughing and couldn't stop—which is a good thing, because I remember days when I cried instead.

Parenting is like *Groundhog Day*: we keep trying over and over and over to get it right. And we believe that if we're successful our kids will have easier, happier and more fulfilled lives. Of course, there is no perfect recipe for a "happy life," but when we're thoughtful and proactive we *can* change and become better versions of ourselves.

John and I know that we're never going to be perfect, but that's one of the things our kids tell us is so great about having us as parents. They say it helps that they can talk to us openly and think through problems or opportunities with us—without us forcing *our* answers on them. We allow them to make their own decisions but are still there to help them process it all from beginning to end.

So John and I keep giving it our best shot each and every day, and remember to laugh along the way.

— 25 —

SCARY STORIES

*Nothing in your experience has been caused by
anything outside of you.*

The Way of Mastery

Not too long ago, John and I went away to San Francisco for a "before the craziness of the holiday begins" weekend. My birthday is in December, and this annual trip that we instituted when the kids were young has always been a perfect excuse for a babysitter and a time to nurture our relationship. We treasure our time together and typically don't have an agenda. We wander around whatever city we're in, have a late breakfast, then either a romantic dinner alone or with friends we haven't seen in a while. We connect, talk about the year that passed and what the year ahead looks like for us.

Because our kids are older now and living in different cities, we created a family group text so we can all "talk" to each other at the same time. Each of the kids participates in the conversations and sends pictures, and afterwards I feel like we've all kind of been together for a bit. The Saturday of our San

Francisco weekend, we were sending pictures of the sights to the family throughout the day. Murphy and Lauren, our two older daughters, both chimed in, sending silly emojis and taking pictures of their activities.

That evening we went out to an event, had fun with friends and got into bed after midnight. At 1:40 a.m. I woke up to go to the restroom. When I climbed back into bed and was reflecting on the wonderful day John and I had had, a small thought popped into my head. I realized that Megan had never responded to the group texts. This was odd, because Megan almost always sends a picture or a one-word response. This time we didn't get anything.

So . . . I lay there allowing that small seed of thought to grow into a full-fledged scary story. It started very small, just as curiosity as to why Megan didn't respond to any of our texts, and it grew, slowly but surely, like a monster in the middle of the night. By 1:54 a.m., only fourteen minutes after I had woken up, I realized that I could text both Megan and her babysitter to make sure everything was okay. It was one of those middle-of-the-night ridiculous thoughts that somehow seems like a reasonable idea.

When they didn't respond, I sent my second text at 2:47 a.m. ·and hoped that the text would wake one of them up so they could text me that everything was okay. Over that tortuous hour, while John slept soundly, I created many scary scenarios around what could have happened to Megan. My heart was pounding with fear, and I became convinced that she wasn't able to communicate with us because something horrible had happened, and then I was so sad, because I love her so much.

The craziest part of this one-hour experience is that at some point I realized these were scary stories that I had made up. When I was a kid, ghost stories scared me so much that I would have to plug my ears at sleepovers—and here I was creating my own. Shortly after I sent the second text, I considered waking John up to give me some alternative story, but I resisted.

Then I remembered I could question my own thoughts and think about other possibilities. Did I really believe the worst-case scenario? Just asking myself the question slowed me down. I *knew* that the sitter was very responsible and that she would have contacted me if something had happened. I also knew that it was more likely that Megan didn't respond to me because she was happy and busy doing fun things. Those were believable and better stories, so surprisingly, in a few minutes I calmed down and fell asleep shortly afterwards.

The absurd amount of fear that we can create when we think of worst-case scenarios can be debilitating. Today, unfortunately, anxiety seems to be much more common than when I was younger, both in kids and adults. Our girls know what a panic attack is because they've had the experience themselves, or they've seen their friends experience it.

It's taken time for me to fully understand that my feelings of panic come from my thinking. In fact, that night when I stayed up worrying about Megan, absolutely *nothing* was different. There was no call, text or event that had changed in my world, so I knew it was all going on in my head. It was only a story I created in my mind, and one that I really believed for a full hour. This is how it works every time.

Our thoughts create our feelings. As soon as we understand that—and then question those thoughts and feelings—we can create new, even better stories without the scary outcomes . . . and sleep through the night.

JUMPING ON THE BED

*Thousands of candles can be lit from a single candle,
and the life of the candle will not be shortened.
Happiness is never decreased by being shared.*

Buddha

One day while I was staying in a hotel with a friend, I came
running from the bathroom and jumped onto the bed. My friend
laughed, because it's funny to see a fifty-five year-old woman
run and flop onto a bed like a kid.

The day had been wonderful. We had connected with a
group of coaches at a workshop and I'd been inspired by all their
stories. Now I was just looking forward to going to bed. I do this
with John sometimes as well. Although John is used to it now, he
still covers his face when I come bounding into bed because there
have been times when I've bonked his head in the process.

When it's time to go to sleep, a feeling of complete
appreciation rushes over me, regardless of how the day turned
out, because it means that I am done with one day and on to the
next.

On good days, I reflect with gratitude on the activities of the day and know that the next day will be filled with unexpected miracles, surprises and adventures. I'm already excited about it.

When the day hasn't been easy, I find the good things that I am grateful for and remind myself that I have another opportunity to take better care of myself, be a good parent, a helpful daughter, an attentive partner or of more service the next day. Regardless, the present day is over; it's a time for reflection and I get to start fresh in the morning. That's a good feeling.

It all started when John and I were first married. Every night was such a thrill because it felt like a sleep-over with my best friend. We would go to bed at the same time and talk until we were too tired to stay awake. The next morning, it was exciting to wake up and see that he was still there next to me.

It reminds me of the delight we see in young kids when each activity is a surprise. I remember wanting to treasure those first few days and years with John because I was worried it wouldn't last. That maybe as I got older I wouldn't have that same feeling of joy. What I didn't know then was that like Dorothy in the Wizard of Oz, it was always up to me to click my heels together to *make* it last. Which it has.

It's possible for all of us to create that feeling that something good is going to happen at any time of the day or night.

When our kids were growing up, there were times when they took themselves and life very seriously and didn't want me to walk them to school, drop them at a party or take them to the beach. That seemed like typical teen behavior, which was okay, but I never stopped jumping on their beds and snuggling with them. They would laugh or squirm, which lightened the mood!

Mornings when they were living at home, I would

sometimes lie on top of them to wake them up or lounge on the bed while saying good night. Sometimes I would sing a "good morning, it's time to wake up" song completely off tune so they couldn't help but lighten up at the absurdity. Most times they would get up on their own, come into the kitchen for breakfast, and I would give them a bear hug with a good-morning kiss. They tell me today that it did—and still does—make them smile at my childlike behavior, because it reminds them to not take life so seriously. Plus, it starts their day feeling lighter.

My clients are often very serious or anxious when they begin their work with me. Life feels very heavy; they talk about having a weight on their shoulders and they often feel like they're trapped in a life that they didn't sign up for. Sometimes they feel that silliness isn't necessary or something they want in their lives, so we talk about how to create that light, joyful innocence in other ways. We work together to embrace life without fear and with more peace.

There have been a few people over the years who have said I'm *too* enthusiastic and optimistic. For some it has seemed insincere and confusing. Friends have asked me whether it's really possible that I am grateful for the day, even when it looked so hard from the outside.

No, I don't always feel that way at first, but I do know that doing something silly can change how I feel, and that helps me to see my situation differently.

Most people want to learn how to live a life filled with joy, peace and gratitude, and I explain to them that jumping on the bed helps me stay in that place. I don't have to sit around trying to figure out if I'm happy or grateful. I just get into action.

— 27 —

Kids Are Like Cake

We delight in the beauty of the butterfly, but rarely admit the changes it has gone through to achieve that beauty.

Maya Angelou

When I'm baking a cake I'm not really sure how it's going to turn out, despite using all the same ingredients and the same oven. I would describe parenting the same way.

Each time I make a cake, I follow the directions, maybe with some modifications here and there if I've already made something similar. I mix together the separate ingredients with a mixer, and then put it in the oven to bake. When I take it out of the oven, it doesn't look anything like the pieces I mixed together. Every time I am surprised by how magical it all seems. Chemistry is like that. It wasn't an easy subject for me when I was in school, and like all science, it feels like it's an invisible force creating the miracle of change.

All of this helps explain how I feel about our kids.

This week I was having a conversation with our oldest daughter, Murphy, about what it was like to have a sister who was special. Murphy's now twenty-four and hasn't lived full-time at home since she left for college, so her reflections were heartwarming. I felt a sense of awe and magic in this conversation that is similar to what I feel when I see the cake appear.

What she recalled were not the long days and nights of her sister crying, the trips we couldn't go on, the times we needed her to babysit instead of going out with her friends or the activities we (and she) couldn't participate in. The beauty in this realization was that those were the things her dad and I heard about when she was living at home, so I was convinced that those would be the memories she held on to. They were such a part of our everyday lives that those kinds of memories would have made perfect sense.

Instead, what she shared was very different. Murphy's memories were about how she felt free because she wasn't ultimately responsible for her sister. Today she says that having Megan in our family has changed us all for the best. We're not so busy racing to get to the next event (because we can't) and we're required to do things more slowly than we might have, were it not for Megan.

Murphy remembers having to really work together as a family, a team, if we wanted to go somewhere—otherwise getting out of the house wouldn't happen. Stories about us getting out the door to get to school or sports activities or to catch a flight, or even about us just sitting down for dinner made us laugh together. Murphy believes that we are so close as a family *because* of Megan, and she values the close family ties we have. Our middle daughter, Lauren, says the same thing.

I'm convinced that, just like a cake, our relationship with our children is only partially about the ingredients that we put into them—after that it's the invisible magic of chemistry. John and I read parenting books, talked to doctors, therapists, advisors, friends and teachers. We used our intuition and we tried things we thought would help our kids become responsible, loving people in this world. If something didn't work, we tried something else, and then something else.

Our intention was and is to be the best parents we can be for all our girls, but we're a work in progress. Coming from a loving place, we try new ingredients constantly, and occasionally we see a glimpse of the cake as it's cooking. Some days we had a lot of parenting guilt when we made decisions based on the family's needs instead of those of Murphy and Lauren, but today it was those decisions that made Murphy feel we were a team. It's so hard when you're parenting to know what the right ingredients are, but that's when it helps to surrender some of the control and let the chemistry do its work.

We're all still cooking until the end, so it's about the ingredients and the invisible things that we cannot see happening in the oven.

What ingredients are you adding to your cake?

— 28 —

LIVING **RIGHT NOW**

What if I can try being Dory? . . . When I show up open and empty, I am right here right now in the present moment. Like falling out of thought and like falling in love.

Steve Chandler

In his book *RIGHT NOW,* Steve Chandler, talks about the movie *Finding Dory.* It's the story of a little fish, voiced by Ellen DeGeneres, who has short-term memory loss. She's forgotten all her past struggles, broken friendships and worries, so everywhere she goes it's a new day filled with wonderful experiences and opportunities.

I'm kind of like Dory, because I have been known to completely forget what movie I've seen, what restaurant I've been to or event I've participated in, where my glasses are, and so on. I don't focus on the specifics of an experience as much as the feeling I am having in the moment, so I can show up empty, embrace the new experience and then move on to the next. This is actually something you can learn to do, and I got lucky to have learned it early from my father.

When John and I recently went out of town with the girls to a ski resort in the mountains, I knew it was one of the best vacations we'd ever had. The trip was a special treat because our older girls are working and it's hard to gather the five of us together in one place for more than a few days. We spent time watching movies, cooking, skiing, standing outside during a snowstorm, treasuring hot chocolate with sprinkles, being goofy, having dance parties, making snowmen and listening to holiday music.

At dinner on our last night, I shared with them that I thought this was one of the best trips we've ever had. When I said that, the whole family laughed and reminded me that I say that every time we go on vacation.

Just this week I met with a doctor who asked me how my memory was, and I jokingly explained that it seemed to be selective. I don't typically forget what books I've read, people's faces, where I've parked my car or what time I'm supposed to be somewhere. But as I said above—movies, restaurants, glasses—all can completely slip my mind.

Maybe when it comes to vacations or to dinner or a movie, it's always one of the best experiences because it's what I'm choosing to do. Rather than *comparing* my current experience with past ones, it's more fun to simply enjoy what I have in the moment.

So this trip we took with the kids was great because we were together and creating connection. Whether it's going on a trip to the mountains, walking along the beach, camping in the desert under the stars or anything in between, they've all been one of the best vacations we've ever had.

These days, the family grins and agrees with me.

— 29 —

DAYS FILLED WITH WONDER

*There is something better than heaven. It is the eternal,
meaningless, infinitely creative mind. It can't stop for time or
space or even joy. It is so brilliant that it will shake what's left of
you to the depths of all-consuming wonder.*

Byron Katie

When our family goes on holiday, whether we're hiking, biking,
swimming or skiing, John and I usually trade off days where one
of us hangs out with Megan, and the other does something with
the older girls. The first day of the ski trip I just mentioned was
my day with Megan. We all arrived at the base of the mountain at
the same time and got our gear on, and then Megan and I said
good-bye to the rest of our family for the five-hour day.

Because it was sunny out, I imagined that a little cold wasn't
going to hold Megan back. At first it didn't. We started slowly,
making sure our boots were comfortable, and we remembered
how to ski. After the third bunny hill (easy) run, Megan wanted
to go in for coffee.

This all sounds perfectly normal, and it is, except for my

thinking . . . Once John took off with the older girls, I began to *think* how this was going to be a "tough" day.

Sure enough, when I started looking at what my day was going to be like, it was already hard because I was envious of John and the girls. I really wanted to be outside, warming up on the slopes and getting exercise with them. Instead, I was inside with Megan having coffee.

When Megan drinks coffee, she tastes it so fully and enjoys it so completely that sometimes it takes her thirty minutes or longer to finish it. This was one of those times. My impatience grew, and when we were finally back on the slopes, I asked her if she would be willing to try another, bit more challenging lift. I wanted to ski something else, and she's a good skier, so I knew she could do it.

She agreed to try, but it didn't turn out well. She fell, couldn't get up easily, cried and wanted to go inside again because it was cold. The experience made me feel sad for her, frustrated with myself that I wasn't being the kind of parent I wanted to be, and embarrassed that I was so selfish.

This time at the cafe, Megan wanted a yogurt with granola for lunch. Most of the time at home, Megan's happy to eat what we serve her and does so without complaint, but when she has a choice, there's deliberation. We stood in line while she looked at every option of yogurt/granola because some had fruit and some didn't. After finally choosing the perfect yogurt, we went to the counter to choose her spoon and napkin and then sat down together at a table. Megan then proceeded to carefully place a single grain of granola on top of the yogurt section she was going to eat.

Watching this very strategic combination of granola and yogurt I burst out laughing at myself, which made her laugh. I began to realize that my day of skiing with Megan was not about exercise or being in the open air. It was about being in the present moment.

With each bite she took I realized that Megan tasted the contrast between the yogurt, fruit and granola; the texture and taste were subtle and she was enjoying them completely. Also with each bite I had been feeling more and more frustrated until an invisible tap on my shoulder reminded me that I had the chance to witness what living entirely in the moment looks like. It's how Megan lives each day, and because I expected something different from her, we had both had a harder morning than we needed to.

Every morning I meditate for at least twenty minutes, and sometimes for more than an hour. It's an amazing time for me. One of the benefits I've really felt from the past seventeen years of consistent meditation is the ability to live in the present.

That's what made me laugh as I sat at the table while Megan ate her yogurt. It had taken me a few hours to realize it, but *I had been wishing for a situation that wasn't possible.*

Once I realized that the day was about loving what is, about loving the present moment, all my frustration went away, and we were both relieved. I told her what I had been thinking and we laughed together at my silliness and enjoyed the rest of the day together. We skied on the bunny slopes and went in a few more times to get warm. It might have been my best day of skiing yet.

The more often I notice when I'm living a life of "things should / could be different than they are," I simultaneously realize I'm not fully present to what is right in front of me. On my "Megan days," I remind myself that I'm happiest when I'm open to all possibilities.

Come to think of it, ANY day when I'm open to all possibilities is a good day.

— 30 —

An Amazing Teacher

It is important that you get clear for yourself that your only access to impacting life is action. The world does not care what you intend, how committed you are, how you feel or what you think, and certainly it has no interest in what you want and don't want. Take a look at life as it is lived and see for yourself that the world only moves for you when you act.

Werner Erhard

Most of us have one or even a few school teachers who remain in our memory as standouts—those people who helped us see our lives and ourselves differently after a year together. In my life there was Mr. Marshall in fifth grade (who helped me see that math was fun), Dr. Frost in seventh-grade biology (who made science come alive), and Ms. Gregory in high school (who opened my eyes to photography and life from an observer's perspective).

Dan Doctor is Megan's high-school choir teacher, and he is a teacher who changes lives. I had heard about Dan and how incredible he was for many years before Megan joined choir in eleventh grade, and every time I witness him interacting with his students I am in awe of how he impacts their lives.

When our girls were in intermediate and high school, *Glee* was a family television show that brought us together each week. We talked about the characters as though they were our friends, and at the dinner table we discussed the important issues they were discussing on the show. For all of us, it was a safe way to talk about relationships, friendships, sexuality, race and teamwork. We sang their songs over and over and laughed about the characters. In every episode, we witnessed Will Schuester, the Glee Club teacher, support his students and help them feel better about just being themselves.

Dan Doctor is like Will Schuester. He gathers together his students from all walks of life to support each other, talk and sing. The students hang out with him at lunch and after school. They care deeply about what he thinks of them and they ask his opinion and advice on anything and everything they can think of. He embraces each of them just the way they are, and they know it.

Thanks to choir, one good friend of Megan's changed in front of our eyes from a shy, introverted young woman to joining Megan and her friends at parties and prom. Having a tribe has changed them, and Dan has provided a space for that. In fact, this is really the first time Megan has been "at home" somewhere at school.

She's comfortable there because Dan makes everyone comfortable with who they are. He doesn't push her to go faster than she's able, and she's encouraged to bring her non-choir friends to lunch in the choir room. There are no tryouts for choir because everyone is welcome. It's diverse and inclusive, and the students produce a spectacular sound with some truly outstanding voices.

Being excellent at what you do is easier when it comes from a place of love, service and passion. Dan told me that he wants everyone to know how singing can make your life better, and to learn it at a young age. He sees possibility in everyone he works with, which makes them shine. It's unconditional acceptance of all students, and when they feel this, that's when they begin to see the possibilities in themselves and their situations that they didn't see before.

As a parent and a leader of groups, when I wonder what it takes to be really inspiring, I look at Dan. I know that if we want our students, kids, partners and employees to feel the same sense of possibility that I felt with Mr. Marshall, or that Megan feels with Mr. Doctor, then we as teachers, parents and leaders need to recognize it begins with accepting people the way they are. When you know you are in a place of safety and you don't *need* to change, growth is easier, and possible for everyone.

When we were young children, we were sponges and learned everything we could without fear. If we can wake that part of us up again and sing, laugh, dance, connect and create from that space, it opens a window that wasn't there before.

When I lead a group, teach a class or work with a team of leaders, we spend time talking about how the common phrase "people don't change" becomes a trap. People *do* change. We see it all the time. When someone inspires me, guides me, deeply listens to me and sees possibility for change that I didn't see, I'm different. I was willing to try a calculus class in high school that I might not have were it not for Mr. Marshall. Megan is willing to sing a solo because Dan Doctor helps her to see that she can.

It's possible for each of us to be Dan Doctor, Mr. Marshall or Ms. Gregory—someone who inspires others and who creates a safe and accepting environment for growth. When you're not being judged, compared to your peers or held up against your "potential," but are instead embraced for who you are completely, you can relax. That's where growth happens. And it's nice to have a teacher, parent, friend or coach available to help when you're ready.

ON
MEDITATION

— 31 —

MY MIND PALACE

I've always liked the time before dawn because there's no one around to remind me who I'm supposed to be, so it's easier to remember who I am.

Brian Andreas

Robin, a dear friend of mine, once told me I was both practical and spiritual. So when a friend of hers wanted help in these two areas of her life, Robin referred her to me.

I share this here because up till now in this book, I have attempted to offer practical tools that have changed my life and the lives of my clients, and I've done this by sharing everyday experiences of the kind that you've probably had yourself. In this next section, I want to share the more overtly spiritual side of me, and I'd like to be as honest with you here as I have been throughout the rest of this book.

This section is about my belief in an invisible, loving, higher power, and how my understanding of and connection to it has developed over the years. If it seems strange at times, realize that it felt that way to me too at first. In fact, I still consider myself a middle-aged businesswoman who "doesn't have these kinds of experiences." But this "strangeness" has enriched my life beyond measure. Even though I don't understand the mystery of our lives, I know through these experiences that we are all connected by an invisible light and an intense love.

My spiritual growth didn't happen all at once; it took place over many years and is still taking place. The progression of my experiences has been slow and sometimes strange.

~

I'd never heard of a "mind palace" until I was in conversation with a young man who was a practicing meditator and coach. The idea of a "*memory* palace" was familiar to me from when I was trying to improve my memory, but this was different. When this young man described a mind palace, I realized that I already "had" one—it was the path I visualized in my meditations, along which I walked through many different rooms and places, saw animals, and met guides. (Throughout this section you'll hear me refer to "seeing" things. More accurately, an idea pops into my head during my meditation; I become fascinated and surrender to it—so much so that a related image forms in my mind.)

Although the concept of a mind palace represented a natural evolution of my meditation practice, it still surprised me to learn that it wasn't uncommon and that other people have had similar experiences. The evolution of my own mind palace has been a very slow, unexpected series of surprising yet natural thoughts appearing in my meditation or while I'm walking on the trails behind our house in the early morning. In my silence, I have new ideas and see new places, which I incorporate into my daily practice. Honestly, I'm not sure how long the process of creating a mind palace took. I've been meditating since 2002, and I haven't kept track of how long I've done one kind of practice before moving on to the next. I've grown from one stage to the next seamlessly. Now, because so many years have passed, the dates are all guesses.

Over the next few chapters I'm going to separate my current meditation into three distinct sections. My intention with this is to have you really experience different parts of my mind palace so you can see the possibilities for your own practice. By this time, you have read the chapter about why I started meditating in the first place. At the end of this book, I've included some of the basic tools I used when I was first starting out. Sometimes I still only focus on my breath or a specific word for my entire meditation, but more often these days I practice what I outline in the chapters that follow.

In brief, I begin with gratitude, love & compassion, and then I take a light shower—as in brilliant, white light. This brings me to a place of peace. If that's all the time I have, I feel full and ready for my day. The second section includes my experiences with my guides and dancing with the universe.

These days however, most of my meditation time is spent in the third section of my mind palace—the Blob.

But more on that later.

— 32 —

GRATITUDE

The single greatest thing you can do to change your life today would be to start being grateful for what you have right now.

Oprah Winfrey

The first part of my mind palace began in 2011 when I heard Dr. Wayne Dyer say that he woke up every morning and said "thank you" three times before starting his day. He went on to say that when he said his thank you, he felt gratitude in all parts of his body. I was so excited by this and realized that I could begin my days this way as well, so I took it to my meditation practice immediately. You can too, if you are so inclined; it's simple.

I say my opening prayer and then, breathing deeply in through my nose, I silently say "thank you." When I breathe out through my nose I feel the "thank you" as gratitude in the core of my body. I do that three times (at least) until I really have a sensation of gratitude.

Really *feeling* that kind of gratitude didn't come naturally at first, so I started by thinking about something I knew I was grateful for. It didn't matter whether it was our dog lying next to me, my bed or one of the kids doing their homework or setting the table or picking their clothes off the floor without a complaint. It might have been the bird I'd seen on a branch earlier, spontaneous laughter, the joy of brushing my teeth, the warmth of the sun or the morning light coming through the windows. With practice, each thing brought a smile to my lips and a warm feeling deep inside.

Any *thought* of gratitude works to help you become aware of the *feeling* of gratitude. If you're truly curious how gratitude *feels* in your body, you can spend some time with it in your meditation. When I work with my clients, I describe this part of the meditation as a feeling that starts in the deepest part of your body. From there it spreads in the same way that a sip of tea first feels warm in your belly and then begins to spread throughout the rest of your body. I imagine that gratitude moves into my arms, down my legs and up through the crown of my head, filling each of my cells completely.

It is possible to feel that gratitude throughout the day as well. When the kids were little, we would start every dinner with the question: "What are you grateful or thankful for today?" And then we'd go around the table. This is still how we begin our Sunday night dinners, whether the entire family is home or it's just me, John and Megan. It gives us a chance to slow down and connect with everyone differently. There were years that we made a list of what we were grateful for before bed so it would be the last thing we thought about before sleep. Other times, we would wake the kids in the morning with comments like, "It's going to be a great day because there's so much to be thankful for today, including . . ." Occasionally I was met with a grunt or moan—and that was my reminder that it was more important than ever to start our days that way.

You don't need to spend months or years feeling that deep sense of gratitude fully like I did, but it's also okay if it takes months or years. For me, each breath in through my nose was filled with gratitude, and each breath out was sitting in that sensation. It was as if my body was becoming accustomed to the new feeling. Eventually I could recall the feeling all day long and access it with a breath whenever I felt the need to.

— 33 —

LOVE

*In my NDE [Near-Death Experience] state, I realized that the
entire universe is composed of unconditional love. Every atom,
molecule, quark and tetraquark, is made of love. I can be
nothing else, because this is my essence and the nature
of the entire universe.*

Anita Moorjani

Gratitude is beautiful, clear and simple. For more than a year I
didn't look for anything different in my meditations. I would sit
for twenty minutes and just feel deep gratitude. It was wonderful,
and still today, some days, I find myself doing just that.

Then, after what I would call a "bad parenting moment"
when I became upset with Megan about how late we were to an
appointment, I asked myself what unconditional love would feel
like. Because I certainly wasn't feeling it.

That's a pretty big question to come out of a bad parenting
moment, and I loved the chance to transform the experience from
a "bad" interaction into a learning, growing and wanting-to-
change interaction. I became curious about where in my life I

experienced unconditional love. Although I deeply loved John and the girls, if I was honest with myself I couldn't really say that it was unconditional. I had hopes, dreams and expectations of John and everyone else in my world.

I have always been curious about unconditional love and spirituality, although I wouldn't have been able to articulate why when I was younger. As a family we went to a local Episcopal church, sang songs, went to Sunday School and talked about God. Today I speculate that I never felt quite settled with this religion because, unbeknownst to me, my father was Jewish. (I didn't learn this until after he died.) Maybe unconsciously I knew something didn't fit, or maybe I was just fascinated by how much people talked about different kinds of religion. Or maybe I just had a "knowing" that there was something bigger than me. Regardless, connection to what people called the Divine interested me.

By the time I was thirteen, I had learned about baptism and I knew that I wanted to be closer to the love people described as God. It seemed natural to ask my parents if I could go through a baptism at our Church. I thought that would be the answer to how to best connect to the universal energy and unconditional love I felt in the world. So I was baptized. Although this felt like a good beginning, it didn't satiate my longing for the connection I knew was possible. I remained curious about other religions and what other people did to connect to Spirit.

Over the years, I have learned a little about Buddhism, Hinduism, Judaism, Christianity, Catholicism and Islam. I know that each of these has its own community and message. I've dragged our family to Laos to feed the Buddhist monks in the streets at five in the morning. We've visited Cambodia to see

Angkor Wat the largest Buddhist temple in the world and traveled to Israel to learn about Christianity and Judaism. We visited the Wailing Wall and walked in the steps of Christ. We've been to India and the Ganges to learn about Hinduism and visited Peru to participate in the festival of the Sun God.

After all that searching for the "right" religion for me to connect to this universal life force, I realized that the answers I was looking for weren't in a religion or a place. Sitting in the gardens of Machu Picchu, Peru, with Megan while John hiked the Inca Trail with the older girls, I came to the epiphany that it didn't matter where I was in the world—I could surrender to the light, God, the universal life force, the unconditional love of the Divine, whenever and wherever I wanted. In that moment, my world began to change.

What this insight meant to me was that I could stop searching and begin to *experience that connection myself.* This was freedom in its truest sense. Once again, I was reminded that I have all I need inside me to be happy and connected.

~

So—back to my meditation practice—I knew that after gratitude, I wanted to feel unconditional love in every cell of my body. I decided to learn from Christ. If you choose to incorporate this aspect of meditation into your own practice, Christ doesn't have to be your vision of unconditional love. The idea is to find what works for you. Some of my clients think of their dogs— which love unconditionally. Others imagine their own picture of a higher power. Some might think of their newborn child, a spiritual figure or a passage in a book. The important thing is to find and feel that powerful love and let it permeate your entire body.

For me, Christ was white light, and because I wanted the unconditional love and the forgiveness that he possessed in so many of the paintings I had seen and stories I had read, it didn't surprise me when he sat with me and held my right hand. Every time I visualized taking Christ's hand, I felt the light in his heart that comes directly from God. The pure light of love.

These days, sometimes Christ is with me; other times I see a bright ball of light in my right hand and I know that it's divine love. Before I ever saw the light in my hand, I spent many days, weeks and years learning from Christ.

If you're interested in trying this, I use a similar exercise to the gratitude part of my practice. As I open my hand to Christ's, I feel the warm feeling you get when holding someone else's hand. I imagine pure love and the light from Source energy pouring into me through my hand. With each breath in I feel the warmth, light and love moving from my hand up my arm and into the place where gratitude already lives, deep in the core of my body.

Since each cell of my body is filled with gratitude from my first few breaths, love can move into those same areas. With every breath I move the light from the center of my being throughout my whole body. For me, it's love spreading like watercolor in a drop of water, seeping into the far recesses of me. By the time I am done with this part of my meditation, light and unconditional love fill every cell of my being.

The realization that I could do this in my meditation was perfectly natural and shocking at the same time. It took me a while of living with this feeling and awareness in my body before I began recognizing it in my day-to-day living. That's a fun (and important) part of meditation because I want to bring more love and gratitude into this world.

One day, instead of Christ next to me it was Megan. All of a sudden everything made sense. It was as though she represented the purity and innocence in all of humanity. In that moment, I understood that everyone is LOVE. When we see another person, it is possible to see their true essence—the divine love that is God. It's who we all are, and in my meditations, I am reminded of that truth.

— 34 —

COMPASSION

At its core, compassion is a response to the inevitable reality of our human condition—our experience of pain and sorrow. Compassion offers the possibility of responding to suffering with understanding, patience and kindness rather than, say, fear and repulsion . . . Compassion may lead to action; it is a readiness to help or wanting to do something ourselves about another person's situation.

Thupten Jinpa, Ph.D.

Christ took my right hand; the next "person" to show up and take my left hand was Buddha.

What few things I know of Buddhism instill in me a sense of compassion for all humanity. Compassion is a "sympathetic consciousness of others' distress together with a desire to alleviate it."[5] One book in particular—*A Fearless Heart*, by Thupten Jinpa, Ph.D. (quoted above)—has served as a profound reminder to me that compassion is critical to our well-being as humans.

---

[5] "Compassion." Merriam-Webster. Accessed March 23, 2019. https://www.merriam-webster.com/dictionary/compassion.

Jinpa is the main English interpreter for the His Holiness the Dalai Lama. His book opened my mind and heart to a deep sense of compassion and helped me understand why developing the "compassion muscles" is so important. (Jinpa also helped create the Compassion Cultivation Training at Stanford University, a groundbreaking program that helps people cultivate compassion for others and for themselves.) Jinpa says compassion is "the very anchor of a happier, less stressful, more fulfilling life and a more stable and peaceful world."

When I meditate, I feel the powerful light from Buddha in my left hand and the complete compassion he represents. I think of things that make me feel compassion: the homeless man I spoke to on the corner, a grieving parent, a sick friend and her family . . . I imagine that the "person" sitting next to me is the body of a man representing all of humanity. Images from Michael Jackson's "Black or White" video come to mind, wherein one face morphs into another and then another—black, white, Asian, old, young, and so on—until we see that we are all one. These are the feelings I draw upon in my meditation.

Once the feeling of compassion is in my hand, however it gets there, I surrender into the feeling, which travels up my arm and into the deepest part of my body. Just like gratitude and love I allow that feeling to settle, however long that takes, and then with each subsequent breath, it spreads to each of my cells.

By the time I conclude this section of my meditation, each of my cells is filled up completely with Gratitude, Love and Compassion.

— 35 —

Taking a Light Shower

*The purpose of art is washing the dust
of daily life off our souls.*

Pablo Picasso

It was peaceful in my meditation, and my insides were full of the warmth I had created with gratitude, love and compassion. I wasn't searching for the "next thing" because I truly didn't *want* any next thing.

Then I had a feeling that Christ and Buddha needed to take me somewhere.

Each took one of my hands and guided me to a door in the sky, quite a distance to the right of where I was sitting. At the door I was instructed to take off my robe and enter the room alone. When I opened the door, I saw and felt a blinding white light that filled the room. It wasn't the soft white light I had so often imagined, but rather a strong, powerful, pure light that I knew immediately was from Source.

By the time I was guided into that room, every cell in my body was filled to the brim with gratitude, love and compassion. I was pure light on the inside, all that energy being held in by my skin. I had the feeling that what needed to happen was that the light in my body had to match the light outside of me.

Standing in the room, absorbing the bright light and love of Source energy, I felt a light shower, starting at the crown of my head and running down my body. It's still what I feel today. It is a shower that rinses away my outside baggage, the heavy burdens I carry as a human here on Earth, and it is as though my skin is washed clean daily. Any story or darkness I feel on the outside is washed down a drain, then down a cord of light to the center of the Earth to be cleaned off, while I remain as pure light in the room. Sometimes this daily light shower has been more like a firehose of light from the heavens—from God or Source—starting at the top of my head and running down through my feet and into the center of the Earth. Other times it's a light mist, and that's all I need for the day.

At the end of my meditation, I feel light, both inside and out, and I have a deeper knowing that we are all connected by this light. When I emerge, I am washed clean, just as Picasso describes in the quote above about the purpose of art; my soul is clean of the "dust of daily life."

Michael Singer, in *The Surrender Experiment,* briefly describes experiencing a pressure on the top of his head while meditating beside a lake. Occasionally, I too feel a tingling, burning, pressure at the top of my head. It is as though in that moment I am completely connected by a cord of light to the unlimited power of the Universe. It's a feeling I sometimes get when I'm working with my clients. I know in that moment that we're in alignment with the light inside both of us.

The room I was guided to has become a reminder that we are

pure light *always*. We forget this because of the "outside" stories we tell ourselves. Inside we never stop being light.

~

This is how I start each and every day, even if I only have a few minutes, because it's critical to how I see the world and how I treat other people.

—36—

My Guides

I get by with a little help from my friends.

John Lennon & Paul McCartney

After this first experience, I would rush to get to the light box during my meditations so I could spend more time there. As with each and every step on this journey that I'd begun with my simple, five-minute meditations, I assumed that whatever I was experiencing at a given time represented the end of the evolution of the mind palace—and then something else would happen.

After many months another door appeared on the opposite side of the light room. Intensely curious as to what was next, I opened it onto one of those science-fiction-movie visions in which a door opens to a view of brilliant stars against a black sky. In that moment, because I was pure light both inside and out, it occurred to me that the light room was a symbol of transformation for me. I went from the human, limited experience where we have fears, disappointment and sadness, to a spiritual, invisible world where anything and everything is possible.

All of a sudden, I felt free of what I thought I knew as my

limitations. Instead I was willing to see something new and to connect to the entire universal experience—whatever that was. For lack of a better comparison, it was as though I had entered a different dimension where I no longer had a human body. I was only consciousness. I was aware that I was still sitting on my cushion in the living room and that I only had a limited amount of time to meditate, but I also knew that this experience was part of something bigger than my mind could possibly understand. It is a place where time isn't relevant, where there are no words necessary, where trust is complete, where connection to everything from the beginning of time seems normal, and where we see that love is more enormous than we allow ourselves to feel on a daily basis.

I often tell my clients that we are pure love and light, and that all of us are connected through powerful Source energy. My friend Amy and I used to talk about God's light emanating from each of us, and how in some way it creates an invisible web that supports us all. People recounting near-death experiences describe being embraced by an intense love, bigger and more powerful than we can even imagine here on Earth, and a knowing that our energy field is connected to everyone else. This is the knowing I had as I opened the door.

At first, I (and I use this pronoun loosely because I knew "I" wasn't me in my body) moved out into the open space and was suspended in the unknown until I brought to mind a specific guided meditation I had had years before. In this particular meditation, my spiritual coach, Barbara Reynolds, instructed me to visualize a walk down a path to meet one of my guides in a cave of my own creation. I hadn't done this before, but she guided me through not only creating the path and cave but also described meeting a guide.

In the cave, I was to sit and experience the guide as a certain color (mine was blue) and then ask for clarity on anything that might be bothering me at the time. It was an exercise in listening to what I often call my inner wisdom, intuition or inner voice. And because the cave was so quiet and comfortable, it made perfect sense that it was my destination after the light room.

After that, every time I meditated I took a light shower then exited through the door on the opposite side of the room, entered the cave and greeted my guide. When I went into the cave I was open and ready to listen to how I could best help bring more love, joy and peace to the world, and from that place serve as many people as possible.

Some days the cave and guide were silent, and I felt that I was pure creation or experiencing the nothingness at the beginning of time. Other days, an idea appeared, and I knew how I could serve someone at a different level or do something else differently. I felt curious, open and peaceful all at the same time.

One day a hawk showed up in the cave during a particularly stressful period in my life. Although I knew by then that no day is inherently better or more stressful than the next, I found it soothing to feel the hawk's strong feathers around me. These days he's not often in the cave but when I need that reassurance that everything is good in the world, he shows up.

~

If it seems like this is all too "far out," I understand. I have been continually fascinated with this process myself. Intellectually, I considered myself (and still do) to be a logical and practical person and these experiences—even though they happened in my "mind's-eye"—didn't fit with the profile I had of myself. On the emotional side of things, though, when thoughts and images appeared, I found myself surrendering to the evolution of goodness and spiritual growth that seemed to be occurring within me.

Several things happened in quick succession over the next few months. I became aware of different guides inhabiting a long row of caves. When looking at the blue guide's cave, I knew that off to the right was a yellow guide who was not so serious. To her right was Mother Earth, Gaia. I understood why the environment was such a huge part of me and that I had been charged to teach the world that we are all connected to the ground we walk on and the sky above us.

I eventually moved to my left and found a powerful, purple guide. He guides me on how to stand strong in my voice and my convictions, to do what's right even when it's not comfortable, to love more deeply and openly, to share this knowing with all of you and to be of more service every day. He combines a grounded humanity with pure Spirit, and I am reminded to take this love out into the world.

I spent days or weeks with each of these guides, learning whatever lessons I needed to learn. As the months passed, animals started showing up. One day, a jaguar appeared and moved with me from the door of the light box to the path to the cave. A wolf stood guard on the right side of the path, and later an owl appeared, then still later a mouse rested at the top of the path. Finally, early in 2018, a lion met me in front of the cave door.

Every time I enter the cave, I bow in gratitude (in my mind) to each of these animals for protecting the space. I have since learned that in some Native American traditions the jaguar symbolizes integrity, the hawk is a messenger reminding us to listen to our intuition and observe our surroundings, the wolf represents a teacher and the owl is a symbol for wisdom. I eventually learned that the mouse was at the top of the path because he could detect light and dark—and he would only allow light into the cave. The lion symbolizes leadership.

For a long time I didn't know anyone who had experienced anything similar to what I was undergoing, so I was reluctant to talk about it with anybody but John, who was extremely gracious—always generously listening and nodding as if what I was describing was completely normal. One day, a friend of his recommended a book that surprised and delighted me: *Journey of Souls: Case Studies of Life Between Lives*, by Dr. Michael Newton. It changed how I saw my meditation journey and mind palace. Newton shares numerous cases of people who, under hypnosis, describe their former lives and what happens after they die. In these twenty-nine accounts, they each feel like they travel to a space filled with unconditional love. While there, they review their immediate past life with their guides, who are also various colors—yellow, blue and purple. I wasn't entirely sure how to interpret the context in which the book sets these people's experiences—life between life. But there were enough similarities between what was happening with me in my meditation and what was happening with them that it felt like the book gave me a kind of independent validation of my unusual experiences.

~

True to form, however, the experiences have not ended here. Beyond the cave of the purple guide is the Blob—and this is where I have been spending most of my time recently. It's where I know that we are all vibrating particles, that we are all pure love and light—Universal Energy, Source and God.

— 37 —

THE BLOB

As information processing machines, our ability to process data about the external world begins at the level of sensory perception. Although most of us are rarely aware of it, our sensory receptors are designed to detect information at the energy level. Because everything around us . . . [is] composed of spinning and vibrating atomic particles, you and I are literally swimming in a turbulent sea of electromagnetic fields. We are part of it . . . To the right mind (hemisphere), no time exists other than the present moment, and each moment is vibrant with sensation . . . the present moment is a time when everything and everyone are connected together as one.

Dr. Jill Bolte Taylor

The above passages and the spectacular book by Harvard neuroanatomist Jill Bolte Taylor—*My Stroke of Insight,* written after she had a massive stroke and underwent extensive rehabilitation—opened for me the door to a new way of thinking about life experiences. What if euphoria and knowing that we're fully connected to everything is something we can all access if we shut down the left hemisphere of our brain for a while? What if when we experience that complete lack of control from our left, logical hemisphere, we are able to connect to Source Energy?

One day I was sitting in meditation, listening to my breathing and open to all possibilities. I had breathed in gratitude, love and compassion, taken the light shower, walked down the path to the caves and was sitting peacefully with the blue guide. All of a sudden I had the feeling that some kind of grey "thing" was in the left area of my open space. Actually, the color wasn't grey—it was something without color, something I couldn't describe even to myself.

What was it?

It didn't have a specific shape. It was tiny, a cloud of fog lingering at the edge of my view. At first I couldn't actually see it; I simply knew it was there, like you might realize someone's watching you when you're sleeping. I called it the Blob.

I was surprised and curious at this new thing in my space, but as I've mentioned, new things often appeared. Only this time was a little different. Previously when something new entered my meditations, I had been able to create a visual picture of it. This time that didn't work.

Every day after I relaxed into my meditation, this fog/Blob showed up. For a while, I assumed it was me—distracted with yet another new idea while meditating—but it didn't go away. So it went for several months, and gradually this once-small fog bank grew larger, occupying more of my space, distracting me.

I was intensely curious as to what the Blob could be. Just the word "blob" is funny, silly, non-descript . . . and yet it is perfect. Nobody has an attachment to a blob. It's hard to like or dislike a blob, which means you can't really judge it. It's free from stereotyping and defining in any particular way. It's not a belief system or a religion. Thinking about it outside my meditation made me laugh.

Finally, I talked about the experience with Barb, who suggested that I simply walk *into* the Blob and see what was there.

And so, with zero expectations and massive curiosity, I entered the Blob.

I knew immediately that I had dissolved into "vibrating atomic particles," the way Jill Bolte Taylor describes. It was as though the "I" and how I defined myself were no longer part of me. The only way I can describe it today is that it was as though I had walked through a transforming doorway into a *knowing* that everything is all the same—that we are pure light, pure love and pure energy.

Because I no longer have form while in the Blob, I'm not even the conscious "me" I transformed into after the light box, I know that I am only vibrating atomic particles. Every single thought and emotion and body part and concept is identical. I am being held, embraced, suspended as though in a sensory deprivation tank where the outer temperature is my inner temperature, and there is no separation. When there, I'm in a place where there is no weight or sound or feeling, only a knowing that I am embraced by all the Source energy and love that exists in the universe.

I am completely calm there. Being in the Blob is where peace and love and the connection to the universe exists. There is no *right* way to connect to love and this miraculous light energy. There is no judgment, no requirement to follow a particular message, no one to compare yourself to. There is only surrender to the profound awareness.

I have been bringing all of this—the Blob, the pure light energy and the fact that we are all one—into my everyday life. That's another part of this adventure. Because my meditation is a daily practice, I don't give myself time to forget. It's a spiritual muscle that I continue to develop and it is becoming how I live my life more and more each day.

I believe you can too. This space is in each of us. It is our connection and opportunity to wake up to the Divine that *is* us.

—38—

IN THE END . . .

*Like a lotus flower, we too have the ability to rise from the mud,
bloom out of the darkness, and radiate into the world.*

Buddha

The lotus flower doesn't bloom out of the mud without help. It is born from a seed, nestled in sand and clay, and nurtured by warm water, sunlight—and the invisible magic at work when they all come together.

We are divine without doing anything. Invisible things are always there supporting us. We already have all the important ingredients, and when we have "a little faith and reverence for things we cannot see," we can find our voice, feel our inner light and change our thinking.

This book is called *Invisible Things* because I hoped to show through each small story I've shared that invisible things are supporting us always, whether we know it or not. Love, compassion, friendship—even the challenges that come our way support our growth into who we really are. I've fully surrendered to a power that's bigger than me, and to a reverence for the invisible. It feels incredible to have Love, Light, Spirit, Source, God and Universal Energy on my side.

When we change the way we see a circumstance or feel differently about a person because our perception has changed, that's an invisible shift in how we interact. When we walk near a running river or smell a flower, we see the invisible work of Mother Nature. When we jump on the bed or sing to our kids it moves something invisible inside of us and makes us lighter and happier. When we give a gift to a friend on our birthday, instead of being focused on what *we* receive, that's a heartwarming invisible energy. And when we don't have labels for someone, that's an invisible sense of freedom to see people as they really are instead of who we think they should be.

When I was able to slow down enough and open my heart and mind to new possibilities, I became curious in a way that I never had been before. I still ask myself questions like:

Where can I stop holding on so tightly to my beliefs and still stay safe?

What small step can I take in the direction I want to go?

What memories have I been holding onto that I can rewrite?

Which of my experiences can I use to help me move forward instead of keeping me in the past?

Where can I make a decision based on my values instead of my ego?

Our values are invisible and yet vital to how we operate in the world. When we begin to question our thinking and how we are living our lives, we begin to hear our own voice and feel our own light.

And that is my hope for you after reading this book. That

you feel more light, that you are more curious about your own voice and that you're willing to question your own thinking about the past and future—and even what you're up to today.

Maybe you found something here you can bring into your family and daily life. Maybe you've come to realize that you are more curious about your own values and whether you're making decisions consistent with them. Maybe you want to start meditating and you've never known where to start. Or maybe you have a special needs child or a depressed parent, and now you know you're not alone.

For the lotus to stay healthy, you have to prune it and keep the pests away. My own pruning involves keeping my thinking healthy. The way I keep pesky thoughts away is to have a daily practice of meditation, eat well, get regular exercise and sleep, read books and watch movies that make my heart happy or teach me something new, and work with my own coach—Steve Chandler.

But you knew that about me already.

What do *you* do to keep the lotus healthy?

In the end, the invisible is the most important part of who we are. It's love, connection, laughter, innovation, creativity, compassion, joy and optimism. It's also frustration, heartache, fear, anger, worry, pain, and everything in between.

It sounds hard to believe, and I didn't know it for most of my life, but with practice, a little faith and an acknowledgement of the invisible forces supporting us, we can live life differently and feel the Divine in everything we do, every conversation we have and everywhere we are.

It gets easier with each passing day.

ACKNOWLEDGEMENTS

Many years ago I used to skip over this section of any book I read, not really understanding how much love and support it takes to get your work out to the world. I feel such a deep sense of gratitude to my family, friends and clients. I just want to say a few special thank you's.

- My incredible husband, John, who has believed in and supported me every step of the way. He has been my partner, my friend and if you've read this far you know the universe was working overtime to find me the perfect mate. No matter what project I'm involved with he's by my side and for that and so much more I am deeply grateful.

- Megan without whom I might not have all these stories. You are my inspiration and guide more often than you know. You love so fully, with such incredible joy, that you remind me what life's about. Thank you for letting me share intimate details of your life with so many, hoping that it will help people we don't even know. Thank you for believing in me when I first started coaching. You said "Mommy, you can do this." I responded with, "I'm not a very good special needs mom. How will I help other people?" You said "You're not a *bad* mom. You can help people." That's all I needed to hear.

- Murphy & Lauren, thank you for graciously allowing me to share our stories with everyone. You have continued to be a source of love and inspiration to me with your curiosity and passion for life. I am so grateful to have you with me on this journey. You are truly amazing women. I am so proud of you and love you more than you know.

- Mom, thank you for your constant support and love. Thank you for reading every chapter over and over and asking me how it's going every time we talk.

- My amazing sister Kym, you have been my business partner, my closest friend, my daily phone companion and a resource for almost everything I've ever needed. Thank you for all of it and for being on this life path with me.

- Steve Chandler, my incredibly generous and supportive coach. Thank you for being my mentor and guide on this coaching (and writing) journey. You lead and love by example and your profound desire to serve as many people as you can is something I continue to strive for every day. You helped me continue to write my stories even when I didn't think I had anything to share. I am deeply grateful to have had the opportunity to be your apprentice, your client and to now call you my friend.

- M6 - Kamin Samuel, Karen Davis, Devon Bandison, Carolyn Freyer-Jones, Mo Baldwin—you are my tribe. Your friendship, love and support inspire me and keep me in the game of life and living life to the fullest.

- Barbara Reynolds, thank you for your love and spiritual guidance over the past four years. You are amazing.

- Kerri Myers & Melissa Ford, thank you for showing me what coaching can be. You were both the perfect coaches for me at the right time. Your love and passion for being of service was my motivation to keep moving forward.

- Michelle, thank you for introducing me to meditation. It changed my life.

- Laura, thank you for introducing me to the coaching profession, for encouraging me to stay with it when I doubted myself, for helping me stretch my wings, for inspiring me to be more creative than I thought possible . . . and for helping me edit this book.

- Amy, thank you for your great work in the world, for being in my life at the right time, for walking with me for so many years and joining me in the divine glory of the Blob.

- Frank, our friendship and conversations have changed me into a better version of myself. I am deeply grateful to have you in my life.

- Sue, thank you for being not only my next door neighbor and my close friend, but for being there with me through it all.

- Peggy, thank you for our walks and talks which fill me up every time and helped make this book happen.

- Karen, Jenny, Robin, Mary, Suzy, Luanne, Annie & Whitney thank you for our many, many years of friendship and support always.

- My clients have opened up to me and shared their lives with me throughout the years. I am deeply grateful for their honesty and desire to live a more loving, more peaceful, richer life. I get to see who they are without all their stories and know we are all divine. They remind me every day why I am a coach and inspire me to keep growing myself.

- On the cover is a picture Lauren took in Patagonia, Argentina, in 2018. Carrie Brito, the cover and web designer for this book, magically changed it into the powerful message of the invisible that I wanted. Thank you for your creativity and work in the world.

- Last but not least, a huge debt of gratitude to Chris Nelson, my editor, who has transformed this manuscript into something deeper and more readable than I ever could have imagined. You kept bringing me back to the message I wanted to share. You are truly amazing at what you do.

IF YOU'RE INTERESTED IN MEDITATION

If you haven't tried meditation before and it seems interesting, I've included a few practical ideas to help you start.

When to Meditate

Scheduling a time to meditate helps make you successful. My family knew how important it was for me to meditate so they didn't interrupt me unless absolutely necessary. Mornings before everyone wakes up work best for me and is an important part of my morning routine. Some people prefer the evenings and some do both morning and evening. If you can put some days together in a row, that's even better because the more you practice, the easier it gets and the better and clearer you feel.

Personally, I have found that a morning ritual is an opportunity for change in your life. To strategically wake up with good words, intentions and thoughts sets up your entire day for more success. The alternative is to have your first thought be someone else's agenda, whether it's the news, Facebook posts or emails. Creation begins first thing in the morning. My clients tell me that this one change has made a huge difference in their lives.

How to Meditate

As I wrote in Chapter 16, meditation is about living in the moment. One of the easiest ways to do this, and the one my friend Michelle suggested I start with, is to simply focus on my breath going in and out of my nostrils for a few minutes a day. Every time you think about something other than your breath, gently remind yourself to come back to the sensation of air going in and out of your nose. Having thoughts appear is completely normal. They are like clouds in the sky, and if you notice them passing by, just go back to the breath without judgement. Some days you may have many thoughts and very little awareness of your breath. Other days you can focus on the breath easily and you have few random thoughts. All of it is absolutely normal.

Also, it helped me at first to stare at a rock or a leaf, or something similar, to keep my focus. And I started with five minutes a day, then gradually worked my way up to twenty minutes or more.

An alternative type of meditation that I have practiced over the years is to focus on one word with every in-breath and the same or a different word on every out-breath. For example, you can say to yourself, "love" with your in-breath and visualize the love of God or Source energy flowing into and all through your body. With the out-breath you can say the word "love" and send love out to your family, community and every person in our world. Or with your in/out breath you could say a different word: "gratitude," "joy," "peace," "compassion," "calm," "healing," "light" . . . whatever words you feel you and the world need in that moment.

Or, rather than a word, with each in/out breath you can count to yourself up to the number nine, and then start over. If you lose track of the number, start over and continue that for as long as you like. Sometimes I try to count to thirty and then start over. If I realize I've forgotten the number I'm on, I just start over again.

How to Sit

It is nice to sit with dignity but your physical position can vary. You can sit up straight with both feet on the floor and your hands resting in your lap or on your knees. You can sit on the floor with your legs crossed. You can do a walking meditation or a lying-down meditation, to name a few. Whatever position you choose, if you imagine a thread of light that goes from the center of the Earth up through your tail bone, along your spine and out through the crown of your head, your body and mind will be uplifted and aligned.

Support for Your Practice

There are some great guided meditation apps that really help. They didn't exist when I first started. You can hear the techniques over and over and there's a structure so all you have to do is sit down and hit play.

Books, classes and workshops help because they give you experience, training, and a place to ask questions, but aren't necessary.

Approaching Your Practice

Be patient and loving with yourself as you learn a new skill. I still feel like a beginner every time I sit down. My intention each morning is to relax into the silence, get comfortable, breathe without expectation and listen to the voice inside me.

And PLEASE don't take meditation or yourself too seriously. There is no failure here, just an experiment to see how you feel, an opportunity to hear a very quiet and powerful voice deep inside yourself—and a chance to experience a little reverence for things you cannot see.

About the Author

Tina Quinn is a public speaker and professional coach to people from all walks of life, including best-selling authors, small business owners, university professors, business and life coaches, senior corporate executives, and recent college graduates. She is deeply devoted to the environment and serves on various non-profit and university boards. In her free time she adventures with her husband of twenty-eight years and their three girls, hikes, meditates, and travels. You can connect with Tina at:

www.tinaquinn.com

Made in the USA
San Bernardino, CA
27 May 2019